The Parental Image

Marie-Louise von Franz, Honorary Patron

**Studies in Jungian Psychology
by Jungian Analysts**

Daryl Sharp, General Editor

THE PARENTAL IMAGE

Its Injury and Reconstruction

A Study in Analytical Psychology

M. ESTHER HARDING, M.D.
Edited by Daryl Sharp

National Library of Canada Cataloguing in Publication

Harding, M. Esther (Mary Esther), 1888-1971
    The parental image: its injury and reconstruction: a study in analytical
    psychology / M. Esther Harding; edited by Daryl Sharp.—3rd ed.

(Studies in Jungian psychology by Jungian analysts; 106)

Includes bibliographical references and index.

ISBN 1-894574-07-9

1. Parental influences. 2. Parent and child.
I. Sharp, Daryl, 1936-   II. Title.   III. Series.

BF723 P25H3 2003   155.9'24   C2003-900481-3

INNER CITY BOOKS
Box 1271, Station Q, Toronto, ON M4T 2P4, Canada

Telephone (416) 927-0355 / FAX (416) 924-1814
Web site: www.innercitybooks.net / E-mail: info@innercitybooks.net

Honorary Patron: Marie-Louise von Franz.
Publisher and General Editor: Daryl Sharp.
Senior Editor: Victoria Cowan.

INNER CITY BOOKS was founded in 1980 to promote the
understanding and practical application of the work of C.G. Jung.

Cover: Threshold Gargoyle and Child (18" x 30"). Publisher's collection.

Printed and bound in Canada by University of Toronto Press Incorporated

CONTENTS

See final page for descriptions of other Inner City Books

Acknowledgments

To the following institutions, publishers and individuals, I make grateful acknowledgment for material quoted in these pages.

To the Bollingen Foundation, for quotations from *The Collected Works of C.G. Jung*, and from works by Erich Neumann.

To the British Museum, for permission to use the lengthy extracts from the Babylonian Creation Legend, as translated by Sidney Smith; and to the Macmillan Company for the material from the translations by Stephen Langdon.

To Pantheon Books, for quotations from C.G. Jung's *Memories, Dreams, Reflections;* to E.J. Brill, Ltd., for passages quoted from *The Gospel According to Thomas;* and to the Abingdon Press, for passages from *The Gospel of Truth.*

To those people who have so kindly given me permission to use unconscious material, and particularly those whose analytic drawings are among the illustrations in this volume, my thanks and appreciation. I also wish to thank Vernon Brooks for his efficient help in preparing the manuscript for publication.

The material in this book was originally used for a series of lectures sponsored by the Analytical Psychology Club of New York City, and a later series sponsored by the Educational Center of St. Louis, Missouri. Some of the material also appeared in the 1949 issue of *Spring,* the annual publication of the Analytical Psychology Club.

M. Esther Harding

Publisher's Note

The first edition of *The Parental Image* was published in 1965 by the C.G. Jung Foundation for Analytical Psychology, New York. A second edition was published in 1993 by Sigo Press, Boston.

This third edition has been completely retyped and re-edited from the Sigo edition, with the addition of some up-dated references.

Inner City Books is grateful to the Trustees of the C.G. Jung Foundation for Analytical Psychology, heir to Dr. Harding's literary works, for this opportunity to present to a wider public one of her most valuable contributions to the field of Jungian psychology.

Daryl Sharp

Foreword

Throughout the history of mankind the "parental image" has been of great importance. It is timely that this vital topic should be examined from the point of view of analytical psychology as found in the experience and writings of C.G. Jung. As early as 1907, with his word association experiment, Jung was able to show evidence of the fact that the parental image has a determining influence on the following generations. Not only is it true, as can be generally observed, that the son of a king becomes a king, and a shoemaker's son a shoemaker, but psychological factors may also recur.

This same phenomenon in natural science came to be understood as the genetically conditioned inheritance which most plants, animals and humans follow. When this concept of heredity was applied to the psychic realm, psychic disturbances were, and still are, treated in such a way as to help people to readjust to outer reality only. The assumption has been that defects must be carried from generation to generation and treatment given only to alleviate some of the suffering of the individual.

However, in biology we became aware of the possibility of mutation occurring either spontaneously or through the influence of the environment. At about the same time modern psychology discovered that changes could occur in the human personality. Hysteria as well as neuroses could be cured. Even psychosis is no longer looked on as being an incurable hereditary illness.

In biology we know that we can only comprehend the nature and goal of a mutation by looking far back into the realm of monocellular structures. Similarly, in psychology we know from the unusual work of C.G. Jung that in dealing with psychically disturbed people we must also consider the most mysterious material—dreams, folklore, legends, fairy tales, mythology and so on—in order to become aware of and able to support the indicated change. All of this mysterious material arises out of the unknown psyche, which we term the "unconscious." It expresses and gives to us, in our own time and conditioned as we are by our historical period, not only an image of how it has happened *in illo tempore,* but also the image of what still takes place in every individual under the specific conditions of one's personal development.

We mostly meet this condition in people where the actual common myth has broken down. This may be a traditional myth of religion, or perhaps one of our time, as for instance, the myth of materialism, efficiency and prosperity, or even the myth of welfare. It has been kept alive throughout many generations and has had life for the parents, but now is no longer really vital to the individual. This produces a conflict situation, and an hysteria, neurosis or psychosis may appear.

The mutation or change required in the personality can take place if, following Freud's famous statement that dreams are the *via regia* to the unconscious, we take the risk and dive into the depths where those mutations are occurring. Then one can understand the inadequacies of the ego in relation to the deepest realities. These realities lead us to the world of myth which tells about the events in the "divine" or archetypal realm and gives the individual, as well as the analyst, not only insights into this realm but also hints concerning the problems with which they must deal.

At the same time we must be aware that our therapeutic approach, as well as our understanding, is conditioned by those fundamental experiences of the concepts and myth of our personal and collective mode of apprehension. And we must realize that, as the author expresses it, "the archetypal images of the culture we have been born into, and the symbols of religion of our fathers, function in exactly the same way."

Dr. M. Esther Harding, in writing this book, has undertaken a very large task. By her psychological interpretation of the *Enuma Elish,* a Babylonian myth of creation, she demonstrates the difficulties as humankind has lived them. These difficulties have been produced by the unconscious and have been repeated in the ritual to allow mankind to experience again and again the pain and the joy of creation, not only of the universe but of humanity itself. It is a story of what happened *in illo tempore*, when man was still allowed to participate in the world of the gods. Psychologically it says, at least in part, that this is what happened to mankind and what still may be significant in an individual's unconscious. A careful observation and deep understanding of these events is a religious experience to those willing to live it. By this a re-creation may occur, not only within the subject but also in his or her surroundings.

In addition, this book also presents carefully selected case material concerning the problem of the injured parental image, its transformation and its restoration to an appropriate place in the inner life of the individual.

I think that for the very problematic times in which we live, we are fortunate to have Dr. Harding's work as a help to the many people seeking a way out of such painful difficulties.

Franz Riklin
Zurich, October 26th, 1964

Introduction

In writing about material in any field of knowledge, the writer always has to face the question of whether to begin at the beginning and explain everything, as one would to someone who knows nothing of the subject, or whether, if one wants to explore the more advanced areas of the subject, it is permissible to take it for granted that the reader is familiar with the ABCs of the matter. In this book I take the latter course, which means that readers may have to consult other works for the terminology and theory of analytical psychology.[1]

More than once I have been told that Jungian analysts are always talking about archetypes and other incomprehensible abstractions, instead of getting down to the real problems the therapist should be tackling—the problems, for instance, of neurosis and delinquency, of human suffering and conflict, that confront us every day. Of course, in dealing with a troubled person who has neurotic symptoms or is in some emotional or moral dilemma—anyone who consults a psychotherapist—the Jungian analyst does not plunge right in and talk about the shadow or the anima, let alone the archetypes of the collective unconscious, any more than the physician enters into a discussion of metabolism with every sufferer of indigestion.

Actually, in my own analytic practice I use technical terms very little, and hardly at all with beginners. At the beginning one is concerned with the difficulties the disturbed person brings, and so starts by trying to unravel the interweaving threads that have contributed to the snarl in his or her life. In some cases this procedure is sufficient to release the person from the impasse, especially if he or she is young; one goes away with new insights and can thereby tackle life more intelligently.

But with many people, especially those who have already lived a considerable part of their lives, this is not enough. Eventually the analyst is obliged to consult the analysand's unconscious for further enlightenment. Many people today, because they already know something about the importance of the unconscious psyche, bring to their first consultation a significant dream or vision they feel bears on their problem. But even so it may be that an exploration of the personal unconscious is enough.

During this part of the work, one is obliged to confront one's shadow—that

---

[1] [Many such works are now available, e.g., those by Jolande Jacobi, Daryl Sharp and Anthony Stevens, and others by Harding herself, listed here in the Bibliography.—Ed.]

other and more unconscious self that we only partly know and that we hate to acknowledge as a part of ourselves.[2] Simply put, the shadow is that representative and personification of the personal unconscious, the region into which all the unacceptable parts of the personal psyche have been repressed. Gradually, as one becomes aware of one's shadow, one is obliged to make some pretty radical adjustments in one's attitudes to life and to oneself, as well as to other people.

Meanwhile, the anima in a man and the animus in a woman are likely to have come into view, necessitating further and more penetrating emotional adjustments. This reeducation of the individual takes considerable time. The amount of difficulty encountered and the degree of maladjustment to be rectified, and indeed the seriousness of the psychological injury, vary considerably from one case to another, but on average this part of the work is not likely to be achieved in less than two years of analysis. Indeed, it may take a good deal longer, for not only does the difficulty of the problem vary greatly from one person to another, but so does the capacity for insight—one's degree of psychological intelligence.

By psychological intelligence I do not mean intellectual intelligence, for they are not the same, nor do they occur to the same degree in any one person. An individual may be intelligent with the head but quite stupid with the heart, and the capacity for psychological insight is in still another dimension.

But bit by bit, as the work of analysis goes on, deeper and more fundamental issues will come to the surface. And this brings us to the subject of this book.

---

[2] [See Harding, "Projection of the Ego and the Shadow," in *The I and the Not-I;* also "The Shadow," *Aion,* CW 9ii. (CW refers throughout to *The Collected Works of C.G. Jung).*—Ed.]

1
The Parental Image
As Source and Container of Life

Behind the individual part of the psyche, which we speak of as the personal unconscious, with its center, the shadow, there lies a deeper stratum of psychic nature that is common to all human beings. Indeed, it is the common substratum of psychic life, much as the instincts form the basis of physical life. The layers of this collective psychic realm are general to all, but they are influenced in their form and functioning by the personal experience of the individual. They are also modified considerably by family and ancestral factors; that is to say, determinants of a phylogenetic as well as those of an ontogenetic nature enter into the inner experience and motivations of each individual.

Indeed, the psychic structure of the human being is based on and determined by underlying patterns, as Jung has demonstrated in his essay "Archetypes of the Collective Unconscious."[3] He showed that these determinants correspond roughly to the patterns that underlie the instincts, and like them are invisible and unconscious. Nevertheless they are inherent in all of us. They are types or patterns of psychic functioning imprinted in the structure of the psyche. They are ancient, indeed archaic, and Jung speaks of them as *archetypes.*

The term archetype is not new. It occurs, as Jung points out in that essay, as early as Philo Judaeus, who refers to the Imago Dei (God-image) as an archetype. Jung cites many other classical writers who have used the same term for the unseen patterns that exist in the psyche.

The archetypes are eternal. We cannot conceive of psychic activity apart from them. They are energic systems of a psychic nature, producing and determining the form of psychic experience. Obviously they can neither be defined nor even described from the conscious point of view, for they reside not in consciousness where they might be seen, but in the unconscious. Yet the conscious psyche is itself always determined by them. Our ways of understanding, our categories of functioning and consequently of thinking, are determined by the archetypes. We are immersed in the structure of the unconscious as a fish is in water. Only a minute segment of the psyche, which we call consciousness, has as yet risen above the surface of the ocean, and from this tiny vantage point we try to understand both the world about us and the inner psychic world.

---

[3] *The Archetypes and the Collective Unconscious,* CW 9i, pars. 1ff.

11

Human experience is dependent on and expresses the patterns imprinted in the psychic structure of the individual. And so it follows that life unfolds according to a pattern, and although there are many differences in human lives and human fates, the working out of the archetypal patterns is clear. We say, for instance, that a novel or a drama is true to life or not, showing that we have an instinctive sense of whether a life story is real, that is, whether it follows or violates the archetypal pattern.

The archetypal patterns are even more clearly expressed and recognized when they are stripped of personal factors and appear in quite general form in myths, legends, fairy tales and folklore, and above all in religious symbols and dogma. These representations give the general picture of those particular archetypal patterns that are active in a group of individuals, or in a society as a whole. But beyond this, the individual has a personal "mythology," expressed in the dreams, visions and fantasies that pass, often hardly noticed, through the background of his or her mind. These reveal the archetypal forms currently activated within this particular individual.

The archetypal images, whether expressed in general form in a religion or a mythology, or occurring as the subjective experience of an individual, are the manifestations in consciousness—the incarnation, as it were—of the archetypal themes. The forms they take for the individual will vary in relation to one's conscious attitude. If the attitude is generally moving toward growth and the fulfillment of one's particular life, the archetypal images will encourage this movement. But if in conscious life one is deviating from one's own true way, the images will become more challenging.

The Chinese would express this psychological fact by saying that one is in *tao* when one's attitude corresponds to the archetypal situation, but that, if one is not in *tao,* then everything goes against one. When one is in *tao* one experiences psychic well-being, expressed as a sense of grace. Jung describes this situation most vividly in his account of his early encounter with a psychic power stronger than his ego.[4] We might almost venture to say that one's fate and well-being depend on the symbols of value that motivate a person. And one can go even further than this, for the fate and history of civilizations also seem to follow a similar law, as Arnold Toynbee has demonstrated in *A Study of History.*

Throughout the ages the function of religion has been to express these patterns in living symbols that not only guide the life of the people, but also have the power to release the energies of the unconscious for conscious life. But when a religion dies, one is cut off from the connection with the source of energy in

---

[4] See Jung, *Memories, Dreams, Reflections,* p. 40.

the unconscious, and the civilization, unless it can find a new expression for its life energy, is threatened with extinction. It is as if the symbols formerly expressed in the religion have been injured and so have lost their power to guide and safeguard us in face of the dynamism of the unconscious.

Now, the archetypes of the unconscious cannot actually be injured. There is nothing psychic, so far as we know, beyond the archetypes, that could injure these eternal psychic patterns. But at times they express themselves in a person's inner feelings, no less than in one's outer life experience, in images of injury, loss or decay. These situations have recurred countless times in the history not only of individuals but of cultures as well. And so it is not surprising to find images, legends and mythologems that deal with this general human experience.

For instance, in Judeo-Christian culture the picture of the paradisiacal state, the nursery of mankind, was marred by the theft of the fruit of the Tree of Knowledge. After that act of disobedience, one part of God's creation was no longer obedient to the law and so was no longer upheld and nurtured by it. Humanity became alienated from God and consequently God no longer appeared as the wholly beneficent creator. Instead, God was perceived as threatening and punitive. So we may say that the image of God as good was injured.

The paradisiacal state pictured in the story of the Garden of Eden corresponds to the mother-world. The garden is a protected space, a container of the immature and helpless child, a psychological womb. An adult should escape from this mother-world by a new birth, but sometimes the mother attraction is so powerful that youth cannot proceed to gain the freedom of maturity.

This situation is represented in many myths, and it may occur also in lived experience when the actual mother cannot let her child leave to become an adult. Instead, her affectionate attachment will seem restrictive and even hostile. This is an almost inevitable result if the mother is possessive and clings to her child out of need. It can also occur when the mother is not possessive but is loving and protective—overprotective.

In the myths that portray this situation the mother is usually represented as a goddess who loves her son dearly and will not let him leave. Rather, she tries to keep him with her as her lover. Usually she succeeds in this and he becomes the son-lover of the mother. In some cases the son remains content with this situation, but in others he rebels or falls in love with a mortal woman. Then either his jealous mother kills him, or in despair he castrates himself, as Attis did when he fell in love with the daughter of a king and his mother Cybele struck him with madness.

This is a not uncommon outcome that occurs not only in myth but also in art and in real life. A son too tenderly loved by his mother may remain psychologically enclosed within her love, quite unable to make a life of his own. He may feel completely blocked and fall into despair, or even take his own life. This is really the story behind many cases of adolescent suicide, where the boy was the darling of his doting mother. It is usually the most promising, the most brilliant or artistic youths whose lives come to such a tragic end. Their values have been fostered by the mother's love and devotion, but often behind her love lies an inordinate need and possessiveness; the mother cannot make the necessary sacrifice of herself, and so her son becomes the sacrificial victim.

There are other myths in which the son does not die; instead he suffers from a wound that never heals usually inflicted by an enemy who represents instinctive nature, the very element that has been repressed in loyalty to the maternal figure. The classic example of this situation occurs in the Grail legend where Amfortas, the guardian of the symbol of the feminine spirit—namely, the Grail—is vowed to perpetual chastity in its service. But he is enticed into a sexual embrace by Kundry, a half-human embodiment of the snake in Paradise. She represents the underside of the feminine principle, the opposite, as it were, of the Grail, and she embodies Amfortas's own instinctive nature, which also surely comes from the mother. Amfortas is discovered lying with Kundry and is wounded by Klingsor, her uncle. His wound will not heal; it breaks out anew every time he celebrates the ritual of the Grail.

This legend reveals a different aspect of the mythologem of injury. Here the figures mother and son are both injured. The Grail, representative of the mother, is injured because its priest can no longer perform its due service, and the son is wounded because of his inner conflict between nature and spirit. In daily life a similar situation can come about through a mother's overindulgence of her son, resulting in his identification with her. It is a pathological situation, but, in conformity with the myth, it may be a necessary step on the path to individuation. The Grail legend is the story of man's redemption as well as of his failure.

So we see that overindulgence on the part of the mother can produce serious injury, not only to the character of the child but also to the notion of motherhood that he carries unconsciously within his psyche. There is also another pattern of injury that can occur to the maternal image the child bears within. It is of a quite different character and results from the experience not of a loving mother, but of the lack of one.

Some children have never known mother-love, have never had the experience of being wanted and valued in their own individual personalities. Naturally such children suffer in their conscious development, and in the unconscious the maternal image is negative and destructive. It is as if for them the earliest image of the maternal has been injured. The very pattern of "mother" is distorted—hostile instead of friendly, cruel instead of kind, death-dealing instead of life-giving. Children who have suffered in this way live in a pathological inner state, for the relation of a child to its mother is of paramount importance in one's development, and when this is negative the child's growth is dwarfed and distorted.

It is indeed of the greatest importance for the welfare of the individual that as a child one should have a strong relation to the nurturing aspect of the mother. Only as one's relation to the personal mother mirrors, as it were, the archetypal Great Mother can one develop in the most favorable way. About this subject Jung writes:

> The mother-child relationship is certainly the deepest and most poignant one we know. . . . It is the absolute experience of our species, an organic truth as unequivocal as the relation of the sexes to one another. Thus there is inherent in the archetype, in the collectively inherited mother-image, the same extraordinary intensity of relationship which instinctively impels the child to cling to its mother. With the passing of the years, the man grows naturally away from the mother—provided, of course, that he is no longer in a condition of almost animal-like primitivity and has attained some degree of consciousness and culture—but he does not outgrow the archetype in the same natural way. . . . If consciousness is at all effective, conscious contents will always be overvalued to the detriment of the unconscious, and from this comes the illusion that in separating from the mother nothing has happened except that one has ceased to be the child of this individual woman. . . . Separation from the mother is sufficient only if the archetype is included, and the same is true of separation from the father.
>
> The development of consciousness and of free will naturally brings with it the possibility of deviating from the archetype and hence from instinct. Once the deviation sets in a dissociation between conscious and unconscious ensues, and then the activity of the unconscious begins. This . . . takes the form of an inner, unconscious fixation which expresses itself only symptomatically, that is, indirectly.[5]

The importance of this statement is not immediately apparent because of Jung's concise and rather abstract way of expressing his thought. He speaks of the separation from an individual's own parents and the psychological implications. This separation can take place either through the growing-up process, resulting in the young person's going away from home, undertaking work in the external world, and in course of time marrying and setting up a home of his own. That is, the separation can be accomplished voluntarily. But if for any reason this task is shirked, then the separation will take place involuntarily and eventually it will befall him in the ordinary course of events, for instance when

---

[5] "Analytical Psychology and 'Weltanschauung,' " *The Structure and Dynamics of the Psyche,* CW 8, pars. 723f.

the parents die. But psychologically, as Jung notes, this is not enough, unless at the same time the young person succeeds in separating from the *archetype* of parent, which corresponds to the childish desire to be cared for and loved.

The development of consciousness and of free will in the adult brings with it the possibility that one may make a personal choice that is not in line with the persistent functioning of the archetype of parent and child. But unless one discovers how to separate from the parent archetype, as well as from the actual human parents, one will not really be free. In conscious orientation he will be his own master, able to make an external adaptation that seems to be quite adult, but in the unconscious he will still be tied to the archetype of parent; that is, he will be childish and at the mercy of impulses arising from the unconscious.

This situation will obviously produce a conflict between consciousness and the unconscious impulses. If one persists in a willed attitude and disregards the inner demands of the archetype, the breach between conscious and unconscious will increase. Eventually the unconscious, which is of course far more powerful than consciousness, will begin to manifest in symptoms—symptoms of neurosis in some cases, or, in others, the individual will become increasingly self-willed and rigid, in compensation for the neglected warnings from within.

In either case, one will remain bound to the parent archetype that then exerts an overwhelming influence, and, because this comes from the unconscious where its cause and source are totally unknown, it will produce an inescapable effect, as if one were under a spell. One may wish to do something, take some attitude consciously decided on, but when the time comes for action one does the exact opposite—as if some magic power were at work.

Jung continues:

> The primitive mind . . . instituted highly important rites . . . puberty-rites and initiation ceremonies, for the quite unmistakable purpose of effecting the separation from the parents by magical means. This institution would be entirely superfluous if the relation to the parents were not felt to be equally magical. . . . The purpose of these rites, however, is not only separation from the parents, but induction into the adult state. There must be no more longing backward glances at childhood, and for this it is necessary that the claims of the injured archetype should be met. This is done by substituting for the intimate relationship with the parents another relationship, namely that with the clan or tribe. . . .
>
> This is the way the primitive, for reasons unknown to him, attempts to fulfil the claims of the archetype. A simple parting from the parents is not sufficient; there must be a drastic ceremony that looks very like sacrifice to the powers . . . . of the archetype. . . .
>
> Our world has long been estranged to these things, though this does not mean

that nature has forfeited any of her power over us. We have merely learnt to undervalue that power. But we find ourselves at something of a loss when we come to the question, what should be our way of dealing with the effects of unconscious contents? For us it can no longer be a matter of primitive rites; that would be an artificial and futile regression. If you put the question to me, I too would be at a loss for an answer. I can only say this much, that for years I have observed in many of my patients the ways they instinctively select in order to meet the demands of the unconscious.[6]

In many, perhaps the majority of cases, this problem works itself out in a fairly satisfactory manner. The average individual finds a reasonable measure of satisfaction in a collective adaptation—work that is not too exacting or too boring, a marriage that judged by conventional standards is all right, enough leisure time to at least feel fortunate. That the work is just *not* boring instead of being stimulating, fulfilling, calling forth all his creative capacities; that the marriage is "all right" instead of being a deeply satisfying and growing relationship; that the leisure is filled with activities to pass the time instead of being joyful or interesting or wonder-provoking experiences—this speaks of the penury of the times, due to the loss of a relation to the deeper values, so characteristic of Western culture today. In his memoirs, Jung wrote:

> The decisive question for man is: Is he related to something infinite or not? That is the telling question of his life. Only if we know that the thing which truly matters is the infinite can we avoid fixing our interest upon futilities, and upon all kinds of goals which are not of real importance.[7]

Some, thoroughly dissatisfied with this superficiality, and others not able to achieve even that much, fall into despair or become hostile. There are those who suffer all their lives from a sense of their own inadequacy; they feel they are unacceptable, doomed to be outsiders barred from normal companionship, that whatever they do will be wrong, whatever they desire will be forbidden. They are accursed, alienated from God and humanity, and also from themselves.

These are the individuals who have never had an adequate experience of mother-love. In childhood they felt they were not wanted, and consequently in them the image of Mother is of a demanding and destructive power. But the archetypal pattern of the Mother as the source of life—described by Jung in the passage quoted above—is not, for that reason, obliterated in them. Inasmuch as it has not been activated by their actual experience, it remains in the unconscious, latent, not even appearing as an image. In the most injured persons, it is

---

[6] Ibid., pars. 725ff.
[7] *Memories, Dreams, Reflections,* p. 325.

not even capable of being projected onto some mother substitute—an aunt, grandmother, nurse or teacher. This positive image, however, does manifest, even in the most deprived individuals, as the *expectation* of Mother. The reciprocal of child *is* mother, its weakness and dependence being the obverse reflection of her strength and care. And so in these individuals, the absence of the mother-image is felt as a lack—the deprivation is felt but not the possibility of fulfillment. The child wanders in the wilderness, and remains not only deprived but also actively hostile to everyone and everything. Not infrequently this despair becomes self-destructive as well.

Among those who go to an analyst for help there are not a few whose relation to their parents has not been "normal," and so their experience of home has been distorted and degraded. They might be said never to have experienced the earthly counterpart of Paradise. This situation is all too common in modern times.

The image of the archetypal parents and of the home is inherent in every individual, having been laid down in the unconscious through the experience of generation after generation. But in addition, as we know full well, these images are modified by the personal experience each one has had of the personal home and parents. The normal archetypal image gives the picture of parental love and care, and of the home as a place of safety and a refuge in time of danger. That is, it may be called normal for one to have an experience of the positive aspect of the parental image. But there is also a negative aspect of this same image that may at times predominate. The nurturing mother may be replaced by her devouring aspect; the kindly and just father may appear as tyrannical and vengeful.

Fortunately, the positive image is the normal and prevailing one. If it had not been so, the species would undoubtedly have died out. More infants would have been devoured than succored, more sons killed than initiated, and so the human race would have perished.

However, in individual cases the influence of the personal parents may be such that the image of the archetypal parents is disturbed. What happens to the picture of the home as a place of safety, and of the parents as defenders and sustainers if the human parents do not want the bother of a child, or are so deeply involved in a desire for their own comfort and convenience that they neglect and exploit the child? They may be so undisciplined that the child's memory of them is linked with fear or anxiety, and associated with anger and violence. What if the child comes home from school to find the door locked, with nowhere to go but the street, regardless of the weather?

For such a child the archetypal image of parent and home will be distorted. Experiences of this kind inevitably have a negative effect on the archetypal image, a disturbance or mutilation of the inner picture of Mother in one's psyche that might be called a pathological injury. Such injuries are at the root of much social unrest and the disturbed behavior, not only of adolescents but also naturally of the adults these disturbed or delinquent children grow up to become.

The community searches for means to control or cure this condition when it leads to antisocial behavior. But there are many less severe cases where the moral fiber of the individual is such that one is able to live an outwardly adapted life—one does not get into trouble with the law, and emotional disturbances show themselves rather in inner conflict, difficulties in relationships or in the symptoms of neurosis. These people make up a considerable proportion of those who seek psychological help from analysts.

We may ask whether there is any real cure for such unfortunate childhood experiences. Must these people be considered hopelessly injured? From my own experience I should say that while there may be some amelioration of the consequences of the injury through conscious understanding and reeducation, there is no chance of a real cure unless the injured archetypal image can itself be reconstructed. The injury represents a serious pathological situation, one that is very different from the "normal" injury to the archetypal mother-child bond that occurs when the child, having outgrown its first infantile dependence, rebels against the mother-rule and sets out on the journey of life. Young adults thus gain their freedom by an act or series of acts that injure the fundamental relationship to the parent. This is a normal occurrence, not pathological.

Having gained a measure of freedom, the individual must then achieve an adaptation to life that is more satisfying than the childish dependence that was renounced. The interest of the adventure and the rewards gained by this effort usually prove fulfilling during the first half of life. But when conscious powers have been fully explored and begin to wane, then the individual becomes increasingly aware of sterility and loneliness. So it then becomes necessary to return to the "mother depths" for renewal. If the archetypal image of Mother, injured by the previous rebellion, can be restored, the individual finds new life. It is as if one were born again. The circle is joined once more and the image of the home is reconstituted. This is symbolized by the image of the uroboros, the mythical tail-eating serpent that encloses the world.[8]

The uroboros represents the continuity of life, the community of the group and above all the wholeness of the individual. It is, in fact, a very widespread

---

[8] The symbol of the uroboros was known in medieval as well as Egyptian alchemy. It is found in Babylon and many other places in the ancient world. It also appears in Plato and the Mandeans, as well as in the sand paintings of the Navajo, and in Africa and Mexico.

symbol representing the one and the all, the Alpha and Omega. Erich Neumann writes:

> This round and this existence in the round, existence in the uroboros, is the symbolic self-representation of the dawn state, showing the infancy both of mankind and of the child.[9]

It is the self-contained primal source of psychic life, really the collective unconscious itself. The first form in which one experiences it is in relation to one's own parents. Neumann called this primal experience of wholeness the maternal and the paternal uroboros, terms that correspond to the mother and father archetypes. These parental images represent the first division of the unknown beginning of things into aspects that are capable of consciousness. Or, to put it the other way around, we can only have any consciousness at all when the primal beginning is divided into opposites, and these secondary forms are always represented as male and female, for to mankind this is the most fundamental pair of opposites.

The first beginning of things, the primal cause, is of course entirely unknown and unknowable, for it precedes our consciousness. We may think in individual terms and speculate about what existed of *me* before I was born or even conceived. Or we may follow the scientists in their quest for the beginnings of life on earth, pushing ever further back into the mystery. Still, we can only guess: was there once a primal beginning, somewhere, sometime?

Many physicists think that this primal source was an energy, but they stop short at the concept of a possible intelligence. Religious thinkers through the ages have tended to postulate intelligence as the primary source. The problem remains unsolved. We must each find the hypothesis most satisfactory to ourselves. It either remains as hypothesis or it must be a matter of revelation, for so far it is an unfathomable mystery.

In the myths and legends humanity has told to explain this mystery, the beginning is usually represented as an unknown potency, a breath that moved over the chaotic waters, as described in Genesis.[10] From this unknowable beginning, no matter in what form it is conceived, the first pair emerges by a sort of birth. In a Greek myth, for instance, Nyx (Night) as a great black-winged bird hovers over the darkness, which is void and without form, and then, unmated, lays an

---

[9] *The Origins and History of Consciousness,* p. 11.

[10] Some other examples are the *En Soph* of Jewish mysticism; the Gnostic story of Nous, the spirit, falling in love with Physis, matter, and becoming inextricably entangled with her in their love embrace; and the Abyss of *The Chaldean Mysteries,* a Gnostic text of the first and second centuries.

egg from which the first pair of gods is born. Here we have the earliest conception of parents.

I am not going to speculate about the unknowable first cause, which would correspond perhaps to the totality of the unconscious, represented by the uroboros, but shall concern myself with that aspect of the archetype which emerges from this first cause, namely the parental archetype, and its connection with humanity. From there I will go on to the question of the hero's struggle to be free of the dominance of the archetypal figure. If he is successful in his efforts he will gain something of value, but the archetypal image will have lost a part of its numinous power. The development of consciousness involves a transgression of the absolute rule, the despotism, really, of the unconscious. Nature no longer rules supreme, for humanity has acquired freedom and some power of choice. That is, the hero's theft of consciousness and free will causes an injury to the archetypal image of the parents, who thereby lose some of their power.

In the Genesis creation story the Garden itself was the mother, while God was the father-creator. Adam and Eve, the first children, were completely contained in this father-mother world. And, except for the second day's work, the creation had been pronounced "good." But the first independent act of Adam and Eve resulted in their acquisition of the knowledge of good *and* evil; that is, they became aware of opposites. The Garden was no longer all good to them; its wholeness had been violated.

The first step, then, in the development of human consciousness and freedom involved a transgression against the law of the parents and separation from them. Humanity gained its freedom, and by the same act cut itself off from the very source of life. From that time on it was burdened with the necessity of making an adaptation in the world and subduing nature to its own purposes.

Most people succeed in doing this, but at midlife one is often impelled to seek again some contact with the unfathomable source of energy and life that lies within the mother-depths of the unconscious. And at certain points of history a whole people may meet with a similar necessity. Unless this task is accomplished, the individual in the first case, or the society in the other, becomes increasingly alienated from the life-giving depths and will fall into despair and decay. The task that must be undertaken by the individual is the search for wholeness, for a direct relation to the supreme value of the inner life; for society, a renewed relation to the values traditionally represented by religious symbols.

Whenever we want to explore a relatively unexplored field of psychology, especially when it concerns the collective unconscious, it is advisable to consult two sources of information. First, we look at the myths that deal with the subject, for they embody the intuitive understanding of age-long experience. Second, we examine the subjective material that arises spontaneously in the experience of modern people, and especially in those undergoing analysis. (Further important data may also be found in the creative products of artists.) If we can correlate the findings derived from these fields of inquiry, it is possible that we may learn something about the problem that will have a certain general validity. I propose to examine material from both these sources.

When in the course of life or in the course of a psychological analysis, we are suddenly confronted with the questions, "Who am I? Where did I come from?" and we begin to search our memory for some clue to the mystery of our being, we find that we have a fairly clear and consecutive picture of events and our environment back to about our tenth or twelfth year. Before that, memory consists in isolated pictures, incidents and situations that we can only draw into a connected whole by the help of family stories and the memory of those who were already adults when we, as yet children, were still taking everything for granted. Beyond this time, that is, before the third or maybe the second year, all is blank.

It is true that certain analysts have stated that with the help of free associations memory can be taken back even to the prenatal period, but I think we cannot really differentiate such so-called memories from the personal mythology which can easily be activated in many persons. These "memories" are really myths, stories of the Garden of Eden state, and stem from the unconscious.

Others may even venture into the still more remote mythology of previous incarnations. A point of significance in this type of so-called memory is that no one in a former incarnation was ever just an ordinary person. He was always a king or a noble, or, if a woman, at least a royal courtesan if not a queen or princess. Now we can hardly suppose that everyone was royal in some previous life, but if we take these "memories" as fantasies of an inner reality, then we can accept them as true. For deep in the unconscious of everyone hides the image of a royal person, the Self, the individual we were meant to be.

In myth and faërie, remoteness in the unconscious is usually represented as remoteness in space and time. The beginning of a fairy tale is always something like "Once upon a time." When we hear that phrase we know we are to be taken into the land of dream, of magic, of faërie and the unconscious, where we shall hear about princesses and kings and the poor boy who performs a heroic deed and so becomes noble. In Gnostic myth, too, every man was once royal, a child of God, and God retained his likeness—that is, his image—in his own keeping, for man was seduced by Error and left the Father's presence to dwell on the earth. Thus dreams or fantasies of having been of royal blood "once upon a time" may not be so far from the truth if they are taken psychologically.

If we probe beyond these memories, or fantasies, and try to discover what preceded them, they fade into the same nothingness we all encounter when we try to pierce the darkness and obscurity out of which our individual human consciousness rose like a miniature sun, to cast its feeble light on the darkness of the unknown.

This original darkness is today called the unconscious, but in the terms used by many religions it is the void, the condition of nothingness that, it is said, existed before the gods came into being. The gods of our infancy are, of course, represented by the parents, who encompass the babe like a world. The infant lies sleeping within their embrace, first as an unborn embryo and later like a child in a fairy tale world—a personal Garden of Eden. The parents thus form an encircling and protective enclosure that represents the maternal and paternal uroboros. We remain thus encompassed until we have won our freedom by a heroic revolt and victory.

By such a revolution, to some degree the individual overcomes dependence on the parents. The personal father and mother are no longer seen as superhuman in wisdom and strength. They have been depotentiated, and perhaps for the first time one realizes they are but mortal people with faults, weaknesses and anxieties, and, too, with desires to "do better." This realization naturally frees the parents from the burden of representing God, which some parents find very heavy indeed. But of course there are others who resent the independence of the child and do all in their power to maintain themselves safely on the pedestal of authority and wisdom that really belongs to the archetypal image of God.

The child's revolt may perhaps be taken quite lightheartedly, for a youngster usually imagines that "getting the better of" mother or father will result in all the privileges of adulthood without any of the responsibilities. The child's unconscious assumption will be that father or mother will still be there to fix any difficulty. But this only means that the child has *not* overcome the archetypal image in the least. Where there is greater realization, the young man or woman may have the greatest apprehension and anxiety when, either in dreams or in reality, it becomes clear that he or she is now stronger than the parents.

If the battle is won on a deeper level and the individual succeeds in overcoming not only the parents but also the childish desire for protection and support, then he or she will start out into the world independently. This will be possible because, by this act, part of the energy of the unconscious has been redeemed from the bondage to the parents, and becomes available to conscious life. In mythological terms, the child has wrested from the gods part of their power to use for human ends. The individual's conscious ego has gained a great prize, but the unconscious itself, manifested in the archetypal image, has suffered a defeat; it has been wounded, mutilated, fragmented. And so the question arises: What happens to the archetypal image when this first form of it has been successfully assaulted by the hubris of the emerging ego?

Much has already been written on the subject of the hero's ordeal and struggle to gain his freedom from the hold of the parents.[11] But there is one aspect of this problem about which little has been said. Most writers and psychologists are concerned, rightly enough, with the history of the hero, who gains his freedom by overcoming and despoiling the paternal or maternal image that has nurtured, embraced and imprisoned him. They are content to record what happens to the individual when he has gained his freedom. They do not usually concern themselves with the related question of what happens to the archetype whose image has been injured.

This problem bears on the question of religious dogma. God is conceived of as the Heavenly Father, or as the all-powerful King and Judge, and this image of the highest value carries the *mana* of the archetype. That is, the archetypal image is still clothed in the imago of the parent. In the dogma of religion this imago is magnified and idealized, so that God is the all-loving, all-just Father of mankind. But in the individual the image of God is colored by the personal experience of the human parents. God is clothed, as it were, in the garments the real parents wore. But the image of God still also carries that portion of psychic energy that has not been incorporated into the individual's conscious personality as a result of the revolt from parental control.

In the majority of cases this is of course a great value, giving meaning and purpose to life. But frequently those who have freed themselves from the parent-world lose touch with the religious values they were taught as children, and do not trouble themselves any further about such matters. It does not occur to them, for this is not generally realized or taught, that the powerful and numinous archetype that was formerly mediated to them through their unconscious psyche, continues to function in themselves and in the world just as it did in the past, while they, having lost the mediating symbol, are left without relation to it and so are completely at its mercy.

Is there any way by which one could gain access to this source of renewal without losing the individual values one has achieved in the world by so much labor?

---

[11] The reader is referred to Jung's *Symbols of Transformation* (CW 5), Erich Neumann's *Origins and History of Consciousness* and Joseph Campbell's *Hero with a Thousand Faces,* which all deal with the problem of the hero's struggle to release himself from the hold of the parental archetype.

In ancient Babylon this problem was reflected both in a myth of creation and in the establishment of an ordered society in which the hero succeeded in prevailing against the all-powerful parent gods. The myth reveals the problem of the relation of the individual to the parents when resolution is sought and found in outer life. When the youth frees himself from the paradise of home sufficiently to find work and marry, he becomes a man, and in this way decreases his dependence on the parents as it affects the extraverted aspect of his life. But as midlife approaches, the problem has to be faced on a deeper level. For many people it is not enough to have a competent outer life. Questions as to the meaning of it all begin to press for answers. And once again ostracism from the paradise in which the Tree of Life grows becomes an urgent problem.

For those who have had a normal childhood, the resolution of this problem up to this stage should not have been too difficult. But for others, whose development has been distorted on account of childhood deprivation, the difficulties are greatly increased. There are also those who have not been seriously deprived in childhood, but in later life have found themselves cast out, as it were, into darkness, ostracized not from the actual parents but from communion with their deepest value, that is, from God. Others, again, experience what St. John of the Cross called the "dark night of the soul," and are compelled to embark on a journey whose goal is so frequently expressed by the image of Paradise, where one may be renewed, reborn from the womb of the Great Mother.

*

After a discussion of the Babylonian myth, modern case material will be presented, showing how separation from the archetypal parents, corresponding to the mythical story, appeared in the dreams of certain people and what kind of experiences led to their emancipation from the stultifying effects of parental control. This control was not exercised in the conscious sphere by the actual parents, but it nevertheless influenced these individuals from within, so that they were helpless to combat it by conscious means. Not until the unconscious itself participated in the movement toward release from the power of the parental archetype were these people able to throw off the tyranny that had hampered them and to become individuals in their own right.

Of course such an act involves an injury to the archetypal image of Mother or Father. It can no longer exist in unbroken wholeness, sole ruler of one's psyche. But when the power of the parents is broken their functions must be carried out in some new way.

These individuals had to go through a dark night of the soul, but once the injury to the archetypal image of the parents was healed, they found that the unconscious no longer appeared to them in a frightening and destructive form. Instead it showed itself as the very source of life and creativity.

In the Babylonian creation myth, we are told that in the beginning there were two entities. They were of a male and female nature, but they were not gods as yet. They were potencies—in modern scientific terms they were energies, much like positive and negative electricity. But from them arose the whole of creation—that is, they were the parents of the gods and from them evolved the entire universe. This was naturally represented as a birth.

When we realize that such a myth expresses the ancient conception of the origin of life, it is not hard to understand the overwhelming power of the human parents. They embody the ability to create; they gave the child life and they represent in their own persons all that existed before the child's birth. No wonder that the actual parents carry for the child the truly magical power of the archetypal image. In the myth, the first potencies give birth to one pair of gods, these in turn to a second pair, and so on, till at last the hero is born. He is a late descendant of the first two potencies, who were not envisaged as human, though the gods, their descendants, were anthropomorphized.

In the Babylonian myth the hero is actually a god, but in later myth cycles, such as the Greek ones, the hero is a half-god, son of a god and a human woman. I know of no myth where a human man who mates with a goddess sires a hero. The child of such a union is either a demon or a half-fairy, a soulless being.

When a god unites with a human woman the resulting child is usually a hero—he is the ideal, superior man, having a god-like spirit in a human body given him by his earthly mother. He is the truly modern man, destined to go beyond the parents, to bring in a new level of civilization. He is the forerunner of a new consciousness, the creator or initiator of a new culture. In order to create something new, the old naturally must be superseded, and the hero who is destined to destroy the old ways is represented in the myth as overcoming and destroying the parent gods, a crime involving guilt and the odium meted out to all innovators.

The early hero-gods were seriously hampered by their dependence on the all-powerful parents. They were their children, bound to them, having no scope for independent activity or initiative. For a time this contented them but eventually a new desire, a necessity even, caused them to struggle against their bondage. They wanted and needed to be free. As a consequence, the parents naturally appeared to be hostile, for they represented the dependence of the children. If the children had consented to remain children and had not begun to struggle, the parents would have been quite content for the status quo to continue indefinitely.

In real life this may be so, but in the myth the parents are shown as actually hostile to their children. The father may even devour his own offspring, as Cronos did when he had been warned that one of his sons was destined some day to dethrone him. But usually the first hostile act is the son's. He kills the father and takes his place. We shall see in our myth how the hero, having overcome the Father God, succeeded in replacing the old order, based solely on the dominance and fiat of the first ruler, by laws which he himself established. The powers and functions of the Father were then divided up among the younger gods who were made responsible, each in his own sphere, for the orderly functioning of the universe. And so the Father's absolute power was diffused.

The functions belonging to this first Father God then devolved on masculine society, carried by kings and priests as well as by the ordinary male members of the group. They range from physical dominance to abstract ideas. This was the origin of patriarchal rule: codes of law, rituals of religion, the rights of property and so forth.

In the case of the Mother Goddess, the problem was rather different and indeed decidedly more difficult, for she was the only source of life. It was she who gave birth to all things, and this function could not be usurped by others or performed by a conscious act of will. To this day Mother Nature, the life-giver, presides over pregnancy and childbirth, and all our technology cannot duplicate her creative function. She was also the bestower of fertility and the giver of the harvest. All down the ages it has been a Mother Goddess who has taken care of this essential realm. The Mother was also the embodiment of the emotions, expressed in the original female potency as undisciplined emotionality, whether in nature as storms, hurricanes or floods, or in human beings as passions of all kinds. And on the positive side she was the source of love and of relationship. So when she was at last conquered, the hero established religious practices and sacrifices by which he hoped to keep her wild nature in some sort of order, and at the same time induce her to bestow her life-giving creative energy on all females, including women, so that they night not be barren but might be endowed with her miraculous power of reproducing after their own kind.

The Babylonian myth thus points up a very important distinction between the character of the masculine principle, represented by the Father God, and the feminine principle, represented by the Mother Goddess. It shows that the masculine realm should be dealt with by conscious intent and will power, and that to a considerable extent it can be so dealt with. And for this reason the education of boys and young men has always stressed the necessity of developing self-discipline and the acceptance of hardship. But the feminine realm is far less amenable to conscious control. The emotions can be repressed by will power, perhaps, but they will not be developed or refined by repression. Thus Logos, the masculine principle, is a matter of consciousness, while Eros, the feminine principle, is much less so.[12]

In a series of lectures on the Dionysian Mysteries, Linda Fierz-David brought out this distinction very clearly.[13] She based her exposition on the frescoes in the Villa of Mysteries in Pompeii and showed that the initiation process of the man differs from that of the woman. The instruction begins in the same way for both, but when the initial instruction is over the man and the woman separate. He remains in an upper chamber where he is initiated by male figures, while she has to traverse a subterranean passage in order to find the dark mystery of Dionysus as phallic god. Then on her return to the upper room she must be purged by castigation of all possessiveness regarding the mystery in which she has participated. In this way she comes to her own true womanhood. This is an emotional experience, not an increase of conscious intellectual understanding as in the case of the man.

In our ordinary lives we are well aware that thinking and all those processes concerned with the masculine sphere of the Fathers are more amenable to consciousness than are the emotions, which belong to the realm of the Mothers. And the Dionysian initiation shows that this realm must be dealt with not by conscious planning and will power, but by religious practices and sacrifices.

At the period of our myth, probably a millennium before the beginning of our era, the problem of the emotions could not be solved—indeed, it has not really been solved even today. However, in the myth a way toward the solution is hinted at, in that it is the "son of the mother" who is sacrificed in order than man might be created—created for the sole purpose that he might serve the gods. This surely is a dim foreshadowing of the Christian mystery of redemption, and of humanity's religious function.

This myth, like so many others, refers to two levels of human experience, the outer and the inner. The first level concerns the actual release of the young from their childish bond to the parents and their struggle to become independent adults. The second level concerns the subjective experience of inner development—the achievement of psychological maturity—by which dependence on outer authority is replaced by a new, individual relation to the mother-depths of the unconscious and to the spiritual values of the Father God. This cannot be established by conscious striving alone. It arises out of the experience of the numinous, corresponding to the mystery initiations undergone by the ancients.

In Genesis, the man and woman took independent action, being lured to do so

---

[12] See Harding, *Woman's Mysteries: Ancient and Modern*, pp. 33f., 38.

[13] [See *Women's Dionysian Initiation: The Villa of Mysteries in Pompeii.*—Ed.]

by the serpent. As a result, they shattered the totalitarian law that had ruled the Garden so successfully. At that point a new pattern came into play. Genesis goes on to tell what happened as a result of this injury—an injury not only to the unitary system of the Garden, but also to the unitary system of humankind.

The original unity had been broken up by the coming of a new principle, namely consciousness. But no mention is made in Genesis of what happened to the Garden of Eden when its unitary state of bliss had been thus rudely interrupted. There is, however, a Jewish legend that tells how God removed the paradisiacal Garden from earth to the hereafter, where it could only be enjoyed by those whose guilt had been expiated and who had succeeded in regaining their lost innocence. In this way the image of Paradise would be reconstructed after its injury. This picture corresponds to the "new Jerusalem" described by St. John the Divine. (Rev. 21:2)[14] But the description he gives us does not correspond exactly to the original Garden, for he tells of a city, not a garden. That is, Paradise is no longer a purely natural product; like a city it has had to be constructed by human effort and ingenuity, for a city is man-made, it does not occur in nature. But once again the miraculous tree grows beside the river, and this tree is for the healing of the nations.

Humanity is also changed. Though we might be forgiven our hubris in stealing the fruit—provided an acceptable sacrifice were made—yet we could not regain our own lost innocence. We might become innocent before the law, but we are now experienced in the knowledge of good and evil, and so can nevermore have the innocence of the unsullied ones—of life before the Fall or of the new-born infant. Of necessity, each of us is a "knowing one," split into opposites. If we were ever to become whole again it must be on a new level.

And so the reconstruction after the injury will not produce a return to the *status quo ante*. Wholeness will necessarily be of a different order. The image of Paradise has been shattered and the Garden has ceased to be a home; it has become a memory of bliss, a blessed state from which we are shut out, something deeply desired and forever denied. Without it we feel deprived, alienated from God and from our original self.

This aspect of the archetype is shown in many creation myths besides the Judaic one, and in all of them the theme of injury exists. It comprises what might be called the normal injury to the archetypal image, for without it no progress is possible. It corresponds to the awakening of the individual to self-awareness. There are various possible outcomes of the situation produced by the coming of consciousness and the power of choice. The emphasis in the corresponding my-

---

[14] [Biblical references are to the King James Version throughout.—Ed.]

thologems falls on different aspects of the situation. Outcast from Paradise, we either remain deprived, forever lamenting the lost joy, the childlike state of freedom from anxiety and from the need for personal initiative in the father-mother world, or we take the stolen freedom of choice and proceed to build a world of our own by personal labor and ingenuity.

If a man who has been separated from the parental world of Paradise by rebellion, or by an act of disobedience corresponding to the theft of the fruit in Eden, is not able to take the necessary further steps to gain his independence, he remains permanently in the wilderness. It is as if the archetypal image of the relation of son and parent had received a pathological injury, so that the mythologem cannot proceed in the normal manner. The son remains in the condition of a struggler, instead of being able to become a hero.[15] This failure to achieve freedom produces a very sad psychological condition, unfortunately not uncommon. It leads to inertia and despair or to violent hostility.

When Adam and Eve stole the apple in Eden, they suffered not only from guilt but more immediately from the loss of the protection and unearned support afforded by the Garden, and—they were terrifyingly alone. Ostracized from God and excluded from the sheltered space where they had lived all their lives, they found themselves confronted by the great uncharted world. Even this was not the sum total of their troubles, for not only were they excluded from the Garden, they were cursed as well—Eve was burdened with childbearing, and Adam was cursed with tilling the land instead of remaining a food-gatherer. They had gained the possibility of developing their own individual consciousness and way of life, though at a great cost.

But the Almighty suffered too, for He lost just that amount of his absolute sovereignty as went into the making of human consciousness and free will. And at the same time He lost His last and greatest creation. Man no longer belonged absolutely to God. He belonged to himself! God had become relative to man. For if man can choose, God is no longer omnipotent, no longer the undisputed sovereign. This development can only be considered an injury to God. Or should we say to the God-image? After the theft from the Tree of Knowledge, God was obliged to change, as he had also to change again during the encounter with Job, as Jung has demonstrated.[16] A further change took place as a result of the incar-

---

[15] See Erich Neumann, *The Great Mother,* p. 66; also Neumann, *Origins,* p. 88.

[16] [See "Answer to Job," *Psychology and Religion: West and East,* CW 11; also Edward F. Edinger, *Transformation of the God-Image: An Elucidation of Jung's* Answer to Job, and *Encounter with the Self: A Jungian Commentary on William Blake's* Illustrations of the Book of Job.—Ed.]

nation of His Son, and still another curtailment of His Absoluteness has been announced in the Catholic Church by the dogmatic promulgation of the Assumption of the Virgin Mary. This has much to do with the problem of the feminine principle that is a major concern of the material we shall consider here.

The gradual change and evolution in the archetypal image of the deity that came about through the increase in human consciousness entails then an injury to the primal archetypal image itself. This, too, is expressed in the further development of the mythologem. It is an injury that occurs, or should, in the psychic experience of every individual person who aspires to be modern, in the sense of one who is in the forefront of civilization and moving into the future.

2
The Babylonian Legend
of the Beginnings of Consciousness

The myth of the overcoming of the parents and their consequent injury has come down to us from the remote past, in the Babylonian legend of creation known as the *Enuma Elish*. The general outline of this legend is rather widely known, but few people other than specialists are familiar with the detailed account that is given in the translation of Sidney Smith, former Assyriologist at the British Museum,[17] and even fewer are aware of the psychological significance of this instructive material. In interpreting the myth I shall rely chiefly on the translation by Smith, but supplementary material will also be used from the translations by Rogers and Langdon.[18]

The legend was recorded in Babylonian days on clay tablets, and parts of several versions have survived. The first fragments were unearthed in the palace and library of Ashurbanipal, in Nineveh, in 1848, and other parts of the same legend have been found since then. These actual tablets existed somewhere about 668-632 B.C. (the approximate date of the disastrous fire that destroyed Ashurbanipal's palace), but the legends they record were much older. Probably they date back to around 2,000 B.C. When the tablets were discovered they were taken to the British Museum, but since no method had as yet been found to decipher the cuneiform script in which they were written, they remained packed away in the Museum cellars and were only translated much later.

Sidney Smith's translation preserves the dramatic quality of the narrative. He tells us that the version he used was probably written on the actual tablets in the British Museum sometime after 800 B.C., but that an inscription dating from 1580 B.C. gives evidence that the story of Marduk was known at that time. Thus the material we have to deal with is very old indeed, and it is remarkable how understandable it is to us now, showing how relatively little we have changed over the centuries.

There are seven tablets of the Babylonian creation myth, dealing with the creation of the world and of man. They are part of the legendary history of the gods and of their exploits, which were recounted in order to emphasize the glory

---

[17] Smith, *The Babylonian Legends of the Creation and the Fight between Bel and the Dragon as Told by Assyrian Tablets from Nineveh.*
[18] Robert Williams Rogers, *The Religion of Babylonia and Assyria;* Stephen Herbert Langdon, *Semitic.*

of the hero-god who rescued the other gods from many a predicament and finally created mankind to serve them. This hero-god was known by a different name in each of the great city-states of Sumeria, Assyria and Babylonia.

In the version Smith uses, Marduk is the hero whose exploits preceded and made possible the coming of humanity onto the cosmic scene. Marduk was the city-god of Babylon. In other cities the same exploits are ascribed to the favorite god of that place. So, for instance, in the city of Shur, the god of the same name held the position in their legends that Marduk did in Babylon, while Enlil held a similar place in Nippur, and so on. About 2,000 B.C., Marduk began to assume greater importance, till he finally became the principle god of the pantheon.

The myth was written in the form of a poem and it was apparently used as the basis of the New Year ritual, which took place at the time of the spring equinox.[19] During the eleven days of the festival the legend was recited in full. The fact that the New Year was celebrated at the spring equinox seems strange to us who celebrate it at the winter solstice, but until 1582 we too kept the New Year on March 25th. The Babylonians noted the particular point in the heavens where the sun rose at the equinox, that is, when the days and nights were of equal length, and calculated the year from that point by reference to the zodiacal signs, which they were the first to map out and name. In this legend we are told how this was done. In Western culture, the signs of the zodiac are still known by the names the Babylonians gave them.

The Babylonian Legend of Creation records the assigning of a particular position in the sky to each god. One of the "cunning plans" that Marduk devised was to establish the gods of his group in these abodes, in place of those who had inhabited them when primal chaos reigned. The epoch when the legend was formulated corresponded to the transition of the spring point from Taurus, the Bull, to Aries, the Ram, or, as it is frequently called, the Lamb.

On a Sumerian seal of about the twenty-fifth century B.C. a god, probably Adad, who corresponds to Marduk, is represented stepping over a bull, while Shamash, the sun, rises attended by his eagle. Ishtar, as the morning star, precedes him.[20] On an altar of Palmyra, dating from about the beginning of the Christian era, Marduk is shown as a naked boy emerging from a cypress tree with a ram on his shoulders. Thus Marduk is here shown as carrying Aries the Ram, the new era, while in the earlier representation he steps over Taurus the Bull, representative of the era that was just passing, namely the transition from

---

[19] [See D. Stephenson Bond, *The Archetype of Renewal: Psychological Reflections on the Aging, Death and Rebirth of the King,* chap. 2, "The Akitu Ceremony."—Ed.]

[20] See Langdon, *Semitic,* p. 60.

Taurus to Aries which took place about 2,000 B.C.[21]

Here we are chiefly interested in the psychological interpretation of the material, and especially in the light these stories throw on the archetypal background of the psyche. In observing how these archetypes influence present-day people, we shall look at the images in which they are represented and their modern equivalents.

The myth relates that in the beginning nothing whatever existed save Apsu, the Abyss of Sweet (that is, fresh) Waters, together with his female counterpart, Tiamat, the Abyss of Bitter (salt) Waters. These legends come from the ancient peoples who lived in the delta land at the head of the Persian Gulf, where both the Tigris and the Euphrates empty into the sea. This was not a well-defined estuary but a huge marsh, for the rivers break up into a multitude of streams in the flat land which is frequently inundated as a result. Apsu thus personifies the Great River and the water that flows from heaven, that is, the rain, while Tiamat is the ocean.

It is interesting to note that the abyss or chaos is here represented by two principles or forms, both of a watery nature, whereas in other myths they are represented as water and earth, or sky and earth. In many myths the primary abyss or void is quite undifferentiated, neither male nor female. The separation into these first opposites is conceived of as the first act of creation. And in our myth, too, the time before the beginning is characterized by the fact that the waters were mingled, not yet separated into Apsu and Tiamat. The poem states that creation started when the heavens were yet unnamed and the two waters mingled, possibly in the marshy region where the Tigris formed a large delta. But the tablets tell us, in this beginning, of the invention of building by making wattle mats to place on the marsh and then piling mud on the wickerwork where it quickly baked into a sort of adobe. The text reads:

> All the lands were sea.
>
> . . . .
>
> Marduk bound a rush mat upon the face of the waters,
> He made dirt, and piled it beside the rush mat.[22]

We see here the difficulty men encountered when they tried to make an account of the time before man came into existence. They had to postulate man or,

---

[21] At the beginning of the Christian era the sun passed into Pisces, the Fishes, and Christ, the Lamb, was slain. The dual sign of the Fishes, equated to Christ and his opposite, the Antichrist, has almost run its course, and we are about to come under the influence of Aquarius, which is also shown on many of the Babylonian reliefs following the Fishes.

[22] Smith, *Babylonian Legends*, p. 8.

as here, a hero-god, even though they stated that he had not as yet been created. We have a similar problem in trying to imagine what it was like before the dawn of our personal consciousness. It is as if when there is no one to know, nothing exists, and consequently, if something does exist, there must be someone who knows it. (This corresponds, of course, to the modern philosophical question of whether or not the world exists if no one knows it.)

So here the poem definitely states that there was nothing but the abyss of waters, and immediately goes on to say what the hero did to bring order. An ego consciousness has to be posited for any account at all to be possible. In Babylon the creation myth was recounted each year, during the ceremonies of the New Year, so that people might remember the gods. We still do the same when we retell the sacred story of our own religion at the appropriate festivals. The worshipers participated emotionally in the happenings they were hearing about and so, in some measure, assimilated into themselves the values achieved before them by the gods and heroes of old. Thus a psychological effect is produced by means of an identification with the ancestors.

In speaking of the Dionysian mystery initiation portrayed in the murals of the Villa dei Mysterii in Pompeii, Linda Fierz-David wrote:

> As long as the old myths were alive for mankind, participation in a mystery cult could be an original experience for the individual, that is, by it the participant could be directly touched through archetypal images, could be deeply affected by them and thereby could be saved from the animal-like collective psyche that is a mere hodge-podge.[23]

Matthew Arnold made a similar observation when considering the situation of an Athenian playgoer in attendance at a performance of the *Oresteia,* the cycle of dramas setting forth the myth of Orestes and his fate. Arnold wrote:

> The terrible old mythic story on which the drama was founded stood, before he entered the theatre, traced in its bare outlines upon the spectator's mind; it stood in his memory, as a group of statuary, faintly seen, at the end of a long and dark vista: then came the Poet, embodying outlines, developing situations, not a word wasted, not a sentiment capriciously thrown in: stroke upon stroke, the drama proceeded: the light deepened upon the group; more and more it revealed itself to the riveted gaze of the spectator: until at last, when the final words were spoken, it stood before him in broad sunlight, a model of immortal beauty.[24]

The spectator would leave the theater deeply impressed, changed, at least to some extent, by the experience in which he had participated, and, as Fierz-David

---

[23] *Women's Dionysian Initiation,* p. 73.
[24] In the Preface to the 1853 edition of *Poems.*

says, "directly touched through the archetypal images," which had been revivified by the art of the poet and the actors.

The recounting of Christian legends—or those of any religion—can have a similar effect, and this is one reason why they form a major part of one's religious education. If the narrator is touched by the archetypal images in the story, the audience will also be seized by them. This is demonstrated annually in the emotional impact of the *Oberammergau* play cycle in Germany, and is similarly experienced by many religious people in the celebration of the Eucharist and the Jewish *seder*, to name only two archetypally significant rituals in the West.

The myth we are considering here is far older than either the Dionysian mysteries or the *Oresteia*. But it, too, told—retold—the myth of the way things are and probably part of it was also enacted at the appropriate festivals. For the participants, the archetypal happenings lived once again and they, too, were changed through the experience. In the initiation chamber of the Villa dei Mysterii at Pompeii, the first scene shows an acolyte reading from a scroll, probably the account of the myth of Dionysus and Ariadne on Naxos, while the postulant listens attentively. But in the subsequent scenes the candidate for initiation participated directly in the sacred ritual, so that the impact of the archetypal happening was enormously increased.

In Christian rituals, the sacred story of redemption unfolds before us, and the initiates share in it through baptism and communion. But for people today, the rites of the Church have lost their *mana.*[25] For those to whom they still express the needs of the unconscious psyche, these rituals can indeed be healing, But for many this is not so. They have to seek out a personal relation to the unconscious, by means of which they can live a redemptive ritual of their own. And for some, at least, the search for the truth within themselves leads to an encounter wherein the archetypal images aroused in their unconscious display the ancient story of rebirth and the way toward individuation. Indeed, it is most important that children and adults should be exposed to myth and ritual, because helpful archetypal images are in this way activated in the unconscious.

The opening sentences of the Babylonian poem attempt to make the participants in the New Year ceremony realize what the world was like before creation, so that they might not only marvel at the work accomplished by the gods and heroes of old, but might also be aroused to undertake similar labors themselves.

In the beginning there was nothing.

---

[25] [Mana is a Melanesian word referring to a bewitching or numinous quality in gods and sacred objects. A "mana-personality" embodies this magical power. See "The Mana-Personality," *Two Essays on Analytical Psychology,* CW 7.—Ed.]

No holy house, no house of the gods in a holy place had yet been made.
No reed had sprung up, no tree had been built . . .
No house had been made. No city had been built.[26]

The names of the cities that had not yet been built are then enumerated. These cities are all very ancient, situated in the south, far from Babylon where the people who wrote the account lived. It was as though, in trying to make people realize the antiquity of the events about to be told, we said, "This all happened before Rome was built. Troy had not yet come into existence. The prehistoric caves in Rhodesia were not inhabited. In the time before *that* was the abyss of darkness."

The myth states that before the time of these ancient, almost forgotten cities there was the Abyss of Bitter Waters, called Tiamat. She was the mother of all creation, and she originated in the place where the ocean was the dominating factor of existence, in the marshlands on the Persian Gulf. But the time came when the dwellers of those early cities in the marsh moved northward and gradually developed the Land of the Two Rivers, as it was called—that is, Assyria—lying between the Euphrates and the Tigris. Then Apsu, the Abyss of Sweet Waters, came to hold a preponderant place in their conceptions. By the time the tablets were inscribed, Tiamat and Apsu are given equal place as originators of creation. In the consciousness of the people who lived on the Gulf, the Mother was recognized first, and later, when a certain stage of development had occurred, the Father came to have first place.

This fits in with the early matriarchal structure of primitive tribes. Patriarchy probably developed only when property came to be individually held, an innovation related to the founding of more or less permanent villages and the art of domesticating animals and tilling the land. And, of course, it also corresponds to the earliest experience of every child. Mother is the first reality, the source of life, warmth and nourishment. Father comes on the scene later.

In the Babylonian myths that have survived, not only were the two waters the very source of life in that hot desert country, but stories of a deluge played an important part as well. These legends may have been based on actual floodings of the rivers, or on inundations from the sea experienced in the remote past down on the Gulf of Persia—flooding that brought disaster and death. So Apsu, the Great River, and Tiamat, the ocean, each had both a beneficent and a baleful aspect. Either of them might, at any time, break the bounds set by the gods and cause a flood that would destroy the people.

It was the gods who set the bounds in this account. God in the Old Testament

---

[26] Smith, *Babylonian Legends,* p. 8.

also sets bounds. For when Yahweh was recounting his achievements to Job, he asked him: "Who shut up the sea with doors, when it brake forth? . . . and set bars and doors, and said, Hitherto shalt thou come, but no further: and here shall thy proud waves be stayed?" (Job 38:8-11) The expected answer, of course, is that Yahweh himself had done it. This suggests that the "waters" preceded his appearance, and that before his time they were quite unbounded. Indeed, the primal pair of the Babylonian myth knew no bounds of their own devising. This corresponds to the fact that in the personal history of each individual, the parents have power as unlimited as Apsu and Tiamat, and also have a corresponding dual quality.

If the personal mother and father are guided solely by maternal and paternal instinct, they themselves set no bounds to their own power in relation to the child—they simply act as instinct dictates. It is true that without their gift of nurture, the life they gave to the child would soon be extinguished; but if either of them exerts an overflowing influence—that is, if there is an excess of parental care—the emerging consciousness of the child may be swamped or even drowned, just as surely as it can be crushed when the parental instinct functions negatively and the parents are cruel or neglectful. So that what is generally considered to be an unusually good home, with indulgent and permissive parents, can actually result in the destruction of the child, its development checked, and all efforts at independence swamped, drowned in kindness.

For the sake of their own psychological development, the parents should make a distinction *within themselves* between the archetypal maternal and paternal roles they are playing and their own humanity as conscious persons. In this way, they set bounds to the unlimited power and demands of instinct; that is, they function in relation to the instinctive urge within, as the gods did toward Tiamat and Apsu (as we shall hear). In this way they can also set bounds in relation to the children, for, as human individuals, they must give due consideration to the needs of their own lives as separate persons, over and above their function as parents.

In relation to their children, too, they must realize that they play a dual role; in doing so, they will help the children to realize this fact. For they carry the function of the primal gods, originators of life, and also of the secondary gods of human fate and emotion, who must set limits to the otherwise unbounded instinct. That is to say, a man or woman who becomes a parent has an archetypal role to play, but this must be bounded by one's human consciousness and personal development. This is like the situation in a psychological analysis, where the analyst also plays a dual role. Because of the transference, the analyst becomes the carrier of the archetypal symbol, whose numinosity arouses in the analysand emotions that are connected with the supreme value; and, at the same time, the analyst is an individual, a human being, with whom the analysand must develop a relationship of mutual understanding.

The statement in the myth that the gods set bounds to the unlimited power of Tiamat and Apsu has another significance of considerable importance. When a person comes into contact with the collective unconscious, it not infrequently happens that dreams and images of dazzling and fascinating power begin to flood into consciousness, sometimes in quite a dangerous way. In order not to be swamped, one must find some way to set bounds to the abundant outpouring of wealth from the unconscious, and this, according to the myth, can only be done by the gods. The gods represent that amount of power one has already wrested from the unconscious, for the flood is not amenable to reason, nor even to intellectual understanding, and certainly it is not obedient to will power. If one has not as yet subdued and disciplined the instinctive drives sufficiently for this task, then one is liable to be swamped, drowned or perhaps inflated, by the very abundance of the unconscious's riches. When this happens, one is rendered impotent and vulnerable. Thus, when the unconscious is activated, when the waters begin to rise, we should look to the dikes and so safeguard our human littleness. Jung, in speaking of the necessity for one to be related to the infinite, warns:

> The feeling for the infinite . . . can be attained only if we are bounded to the utmost. The greatest limitation for man is the "self"; it is manifested in the experience: "I am *only* that!" Only consciousness of our narrow confinement in the self forms the link to the limitlessness of the unconscious. . . . In knowing ourselves to be unique in our personal combination—that is, ultimately limited—we possess also the capacity for becoming conscious of the infinite. But only then![27]

Otherwise, the waters of the deluge can overwhelm us.

When the Babylonians reenacted this myth at the New Year, they reminded the people of the necessity to limit or control the workings of Tiamat and Apsu. This evoked in them the will to do as the hero of old had done, and so gain their own freedom. And in a similar way, in times when the unconscious threatens to overwhelm us, myths and legends, especially of our own religious roots, may evoke the helpful symbol that can set bounds to the invading floods.

True, the waters of the unconscious can threaten to swamp us, but we dare not seek to check them altogether, for without their nourishing stream life becomes arid and we perish. The Babylonians used a hymn, ancient even in their own day, as a prayer to the river, which is here hailed as a goddess.

---

[27] *Memories, Dreams, Reflections,* p. 325.

> Thou River, creatress of all things,
> When the great gods dug thee, on thy bank they placed Mercy;
> Within thee, Ea, king of the Apsu, built his abode.
> They gave thee the Flood, the unequalled.
> Fire, rage, splendor and terror,
> Ea and Marduk gave thee.
> Thou judgest the judgment of men.
> O great River, far-famed River, River of the sanctuaries,
> Thy waters are release: receive from me my prayer.[28]

In this prayer the river deity is said to have the power of the flood, of rage, splendor and terror. Then the poem adds that the river judges humanity. Of course, this is objectively true. We build our dikes and the river judges them, showing whether they are built well or are of shoddy workmanship. Similarly, we build our psychological dikes and conscious ego-house, which are then tested by the river of the unconscious. The river shows whether the structure is capable of standing against the onslaught of the enraged Apsu. Likewise, when, for instance, the conventional ways of society have broken down, can one stand firm in oneself, safe from disintegration? This is the test by the river; the test of the strength of reality is always part of the ordeal. It is a test that many people have had to undergo, not only in concentration camps and in war-ruined cities, but also wherever moral customs and conventions are undergoing more or less drastic change.

Yet the hymn continues, "O great River, thy waters are release," and ends with the petition, "receive from me my prayer." Apparently, even in those faraway days, this very modern problem was already present. Our house had become a prison, as our too rational consciousness has become today, and we needed then, as we do now, the release that only the waters of the great river could give.

After this introduction and apotropaic prayer, the poem goes on to narrate the primal happenings. In the beginning, according to Berosus in his *History of Babylonia,* "there existed nothing but darkness, and an abyss of waters."[29] A Sumerian poem, most of which has been lost, describes what happened then:

> In a day of antiquity, when they created Heaven and Earth,
> In a night of antiquity, when they created Heaven and Earth.[30]

---

[28] Langdon, *Semitic,* p. 105.
[29] Quoted in Smith, *Babylonian Legends,* p. 11. Berosus was a priest of Bel-Marduk, that is, the Lord Marduk, in Babylon about 280 B.C.
[30] Langdon, *Semitic,* p. 289.

The opening lines of our text attempt to convey a similar scene of the nothing-ness out of which the world was created:

> When on high the heavens were not named. . . .

—implying that nothing whatever existed before the gods conceived its form and gave it a name. Then Apsu, the underworld fresh-water sea, the primal engenderer of all things, united with Tiamat, the salt sea, "Bearer of all."

It is interesting to see how the Babylonians traced everything not to a single supreme being from whom the pairs arose, as most of the great religions do, but to a pair opposite in nature—one male, the other female. Apsu, the fresh water, was the male principle and the water of life, essential to all living things. He is generally represented in Babylonian art as an overflowing bowl, descending from heaven, often in the hands of an angel. But Tiamat, the salt water, was the originator of life, whose saltiness corresponded to the juices of all creatures. Their blood and tears and the waters of the womb, set free in childbirth, are all salty and came from Tiamat, mother of all gods and demons, and of all life.

Although these two primal beings had such different functions, they were yet alike in that they were both of a watery nature—both chaotic and dark—each hating to be disturbed, especially by a new principle that might impose order and thereby limit their boundless freedom.

Tiamat probably represented the primal state that is described in Genesis as being void and without form. In the much later Chaldean Mysteries this primal state is spoken of simply as the Abyss, or the Depths. Tiamat is represented as a dragon (Figure 1), or a monstrously horned serpent. Apsu is not personified in Babylonian art, but is represented by the vase of overflowing water (Figure 2), as mentioned above. Apsu and Tiamat, then, were the original watery chaos that is today called the collective unconscious, which is itself the source and origin of all psychic life. With these original two, we are told, there was another, Mummu, their chamberlain or messenger. The Babylonians say that *mummu* meant "the word" or "the utterance," and Langdon translates it as "intelligence" or "effectivity."[31] So Mummu corresponds roughly to Logos.

Already, probably as far back as 2,000 B.C., the void that corresponds to what we would call the collective unconscious was conceived of as separated into two parts, opposites, two creatures or potencies that were possessed of a sort of consciousness, which had come about, perhaps, just because the void had already been separated into opposites. At least, we are told that they were ac-companied by an intelligence, a word, called Mummu. This situation reminds us

---

[31] Ibid., p. 290.

Figure 1. Tiamat, represented as a dragon.
(From Sidney Smith, *The Babylonian Legends of the Creation*)

Figure 2. Apsu, represented by a vase of overflowing water.
(From Stephen Langdon, *Semitic*)

of how Jung, in his "Answer to Job," repeatedly points out that Yahweh had an intelligence, conceived of as a separate person within the deity, but that he repeatedly failed to consult with this intelligence, which might have informed him of certain things he was overlooking.[32]

In the case of Apsu and Tiamat, this intelligence functioned like a fiat, emerging out of the depths of the unknown and unknowable abyss, that gave utterance to the way things *had to be*. It was the creative utterance of a god that causes whatever is spoken to come into being. The creation myth in Genesis starts in this same way, with just such a spoken fiat: "God said, Let there be light: and there was light." (1:3)

It is interesting to find this conception of an intelligence in the chaotic abyss. It corresponds to Jung's insistence that dreams have meaning and show consciousness of a sort within the unconscious. It is as if there were light sparks in the darkness. These are the so-called fish eyes shining in the ocean that Jung equates to archetypal images in dreams. He quotes Hyppolytus, who states that the darkness held "the brightness and the spark of light in thrall," and that this "very small spark" was finely mingled in the dark waters below.[33]

Mummu is such an unconscious consciousness. He seems to be more directly connected with Apsu than with Tiamat. For Apsu is the male principle that includes consciousness and thinking. He is the active part of the primal chaos, while Tiamat, his spouse, is the bearer of life, but is without this spark of light, for she is abysmal darkness and instinctive emotionality. However, it is she who possesses the Tablet of Destinies. That is to say, "fate" is in the hands of emotional factors that are considered to be primitive—they are not under the control and guidance of rational and intellectual powers. This is an insight found down through the ages. For the Fates, who spin or weave the entangling web of life, are always women. The Norns of Nordic myth and the Spinning Woman of Navaho mythology are examples, and there are many others.

In Babylon, the Tablet of Destinies was conceived of as a sort of amulet, worn about the neck. On it were inscribed the fates of all living beings, including the gods. It also spelled out the runes of all happenings. It originally belonged to Tiamat, the mother-potency, but during the course of our story it passed into other hands, with fateful consequences for mankind, for the power to determine the fates belonged to whoever wore the Tablet. This person became, in a sense, an absolute tyrant, with far greater power than any earthly ruler.

This Tablet plays a significant part in the story of the hero's struggle to gain

---

[32] *Psychology and Religion*, CW 11, pars. 560ff.

[33] *Aion*, CW 9ii, par. 344.

freedom from the absolute power of Apsu and Tiamat, and the later gods. The whole problem of destiny and free will is bound up with the struggle to possess the Tablet, a struggle that was eventually resolved, in Babylon, on a religious basis. When Apsu was killed, his power was divided among the younger gods. His name was given to the temple and sanctuary of Ea, Lord of the Waters, and Apsu, as a deity, disappeared from the scene. But Tiamat could not be so easily disposed of. The resolution of the problem of the emotional part of the psyche that she represents needed a religious attitude and a ritual which, in our myth, was accompanied by sacrifices, as indeed is usually the case. In the Babylonian myth the reason why this is so is given. Human fate hangs on the possession of the Tablet of Destinies. We can have no say in our own destiny, no control of our fate by free will, unless we pay tribute to the power that still possesses the Tablet. In practical language, so long as we do not have a religious attitude in regard to the passionate emotions that well up in us, we hand our fate over to that blind despot whom the Babylonians called Tiamat.

The struggle against Apsu and Tiamat, the monsters of chaos, was undertaken in order to release the world from the arbitrary rule of the unconscious, and to institute a new order. This struggle was begun by the first gods, who were the children of the primal pair, and carried on by the younger gods. And eventually the heroes, forerunners of our own heroic potential, had to take responsibility for completing the task that had been begun by the gods. That is, the struggle against arbitrary fate was first carried out only by instinctive reactions arising from the unconscious, symbolized by the gods. But when this instinctive ordering encounters the emotional realm, only a hero—a heroic element in humans themselves, having consciousness and the ability to plan a campaign—can have any chance of success.

This mythologem corresponds to the development of consciousness in the human being. In the earliest stages of the dawn of consciousness, the infant is controlled by primal forces, represented by the powerful parents. At this stage the individual is still unconscious of what he or she is doing and why, for the ego-complex has not yet emerged into consciousness and one's reactions are purely instinctive. It is only a good deal later, when self-awareness emerges as "I," that it is possible to take up the hero struggle, to stick out one's jaw and make a fist and say, "I won't!"—perhaps to some rule that, up till then, has been accepted as unalterable.

This rebellion goes on throughout childhood and adolescence, with increasing insight and power of adaptation, until around twenty or twenty-five when the youth becomes an adult, ready to take on adult responsibilities and self-determination. But this outer victory over the personal parents does not necessarily, or even usually, imply release from the archetypal parents. For this, if genuine freedom is to be gained, further development is needed.

This is why some individuals undertake the inner, subjective task of the hero—namely, to free consciousness from the domination of unconscious forces. In the course of the struggle, as told in the Babylonian myth, the Tablet, being always the first prize of victory, passed from one person to another. When one of the demons possessed it, all fates were decreed by him—that is, humanity suffered an evil fate, and all were compelled by unconscious forces to do evil, even though in consciousness they might intend to do good. Just as, when all want peace, an evil fate pushes them into war. On the other hand, when a hero-god secured the Tablet, he in turn determined the course of events.

By the time our poem was written, the Tablet had become part of the sacred treasure of the temple, and each year all the gods of the pantheon sat in solemn conclave and determined the destinies for the coming year; that is to say, the fate of the world was determined by a parliament of gods—humanity, of course, was not consulted! The destinies were made known through the casting of horoscopes, for the gods were associated with the constellations and the stars, where they were thought to have their abode. To this day, the planets and constellations are called by the names of gods and heroes. On a tablet dealing with this matter, it was said: "Only the stars change not eternally; they determine day and night and indicate the times of the festivals exactly."[34] Yet—and this is one of the rare places in cuneiform literature where man's freedom of will is even hinted at—it was decreed that men should have some power to make their own plans: "the skilled for the skilled, the fool for the fool."[35]

A similar recognition of man's relative freedom and autonomy in face of the immutable laws of fate is taught in the *I Ching,* a Chinese text dating from about the same period as our myth. The commentaries on the oracular sayings are based on age-old Chinese wisdom teachings, and regarding Hexagram 15 (Modesty) we read:

> The destinies of men are subject to immutable laws that must fulfill themselves. But man has it in his power to shape his fate, according as his behavior exposes him to the influence of benevolent or of destructive forces.[36]

This corresponds to the teaching of the Babylonian myth that humanity must study the situation and disposition of the gods religiously and be guided according to their indications. For it is only by careful attention that we can learn

---

[34] Langdon, *Semitic,* p. 314.
[35] Ibid.
[36] *The I Ching or Book of Changes,* p. 64.

how to adapt to the times so as to cooperate with the divine powers and avoid disaster. In ancient Babylon this was done by a religious casting of horoscopes in order to determine the position and disposition of the gods. In the present, we must also observe with scrupulous care the indications that come from the unconscious. The Tablet of Destinies is carried for us, as for the ancients, by unseen forces and powers—the *factors,* the *doers*—who act behind the scenes and determine our fate without our knowledge. If we pay attention to the intimations from the unconscious we may learn how to adapt to the psychic situation unfolding in the unconscious, foreshadowing future events.

In the case of the individual, dreams may also give an indication of unconscious trends, while on a broader scale mythologems indicate the pattern in which events have unfolded in the past. And so, when an archetypal pattern is constellated and becomes active in either an individual or a people, the related myth may give an indication of the way in which events will unfold.

The mythologems represent the archetypal patterns that underlie the development of history, but they also underlie the development of human consciousness in its particular form in each individual. Our chief interest in the ancient stories and cosmogonic myths stems from the fact that while they give legendary accounts of the beginnings of the world, they are also records of the gradual evolution of consciousness in man. They contain, as it were, the history of man's experience vis-à-vis life with all its problems as well as its fulfillments, whether these be inner or outer. The age-old experiences of the human race have left imprints in the capacities of individuals—inborn patterns of behavior that we call instincts. In addition, there are patterns of functioning in the psyche that express themselves in images and are recorded in many forms of story.

These inborn patterns, or archetypes, are of course inaccessible to consciousness, but their *images* are readily observed and, indeed, they underlie our dreams, our fantasies, and our understanding of other people, as well as of life itself. The motifs of legend, myths and fairy tales also correspond to archetypal patterns, so that when we study a myth, for instance, we are at the same time observing how humanity has dealt with the unconscious, in which we were originally embedded, and how, through courage, growing awareness and initiative, we have won the freedom to become individuals in our own right.

The opening words of the Babylonian myth relate that the chaos of uncreated beginning had already been split into opposites and had taken the form of two potencies, Apsu and Tiamat. In psychological terms, these two original beings are the primary archetypal images of the collective unconscious. When our story starts they were the only beings that had as yet come into existence. So it seems that Apsu and Tiamat were separate from one another in the beginning, and only later mingled their waters. This intermingling was the beginning of a change; in a sense, it was the beginning of history. The mingling of their waters is like a marriage of the primal opposites that results in the birth of a new order, and can, perhaps, be equated to the Gnostic legend of the marriage between Nous and Physis—spirit and matter.

The poem describes this first step in creation as follows:

> When the heavens above were yet unnamed,
> And no dwelling beneath was called by a name,
> Apsu, the oldest of beings, their progenitor,
> Mummu, Tiamat, who bare each and all of them—
> Mingled their waters into a single mass.
> No steady terrace had been constructed, no marsh had been searched out,
> When none of the gods had been brought into being,
> No names had been recorded, no fates had been fixed,
> The gods came into being within them.
> . . . they were named.[37]

Apsu, we are told, was the oldest being, the progenitor of the gods, while Tiamat was female, the mother who bore them. But, as yet, nothing had been named—not even the heavens. Then the gods came into being, within the first parents, and were named.

The emphasis on the giving of names is important, for the name of an object, in primitive thinking, *is* the object itself, or its ghost, its spirit. It was even believed that nothing could exist apart from its name, while to know the name gave one magic power over the object. Many ancient papyri consist of lists of names, knowledge of which would impart power—the power to invoke a deity and so command his assistance. Similarly, a magician wields power over the genie by virtue of knowing its name. For this reason, a man's initiation name— that is, his real, individual name—was frequently kept secret for fear that some evilly disposed person might use it to compel obedience or inflict injury. In a certain sense, the name *is* the person. This very primitive idea corresponds to a psychological truth and fits in with a philosophical theory, namely that an object or act only exists for a person if he or she can name it, that is, if one is conscious of its nature. It also accounts for the frustration we often feel when we cannot remember the name of something. It is as if we had lost our relation to it and consequently are helpless before it. So, the first step in consciousness and the gaining of power in the world is the naming of things.

You will recall that the first recorded act of Adam and Eve was to name the

---

[37] Smith, *Babylonian Legends,* pp. 34f.

animals, a feat of which the animals themselves were incapable. In the development of children, the learning of names is an obvious first step toward consciousness and a sense of competence. As adults, if we do not give names to things, we cannot remember them or relate them to other already known objects. This also holds true in regard to any new observation. For instance, parapsychological and synchronistic phenomena have presumably always occurred, but, from the scientific point of view, they were not respectable; they were dismissed as fantasies, if not actual trickery. Only when Rhine and then Jung gave them a name did scientists begin to be willing to investigate them.

So here the poem is tacitly implying that chaos, or unconsciousness, continued in complete control of the universe until the power of naming arose. In the Babylonian legend this was the work of Mummu, the intelligent Word, really the Logos. He is mentioned here, but his activity is glossed over. His name just emerges between those of Apsu and Tiamat.

Up to this point in the myth, the first beings were said to be abysses of water, but now they are named, given, as it were, personal names. Immediately after we are told a story of their doings, as if they had a biography—they become personalized. This is exactly what happens in active imagination when we engage in dialogue with a mood or other unconscious part of the psyche. We personify it, give it a name, or, more likely, it tells us its own name; then the mythical story can begin to unfold, with the result that consciousness is enlarged by the inclusion of a previously unknown part of the psyche.

In the myth, the process of creation went on for countless ages, during which the primary pair gave birth to the gods. Finally the three gods emerged: Anu, Enlil and Ea, the great trinity of the Assyrian and Babylonian pantheon. Anu was god of the highest heaven. The bread and water of eternal life and the plant of birth or of immortality were in his keeping. The middle world was the abode of Enlil, the earth god. He was Lord of the Winds, which were believed to reside in a cave. The lowest world, the place of the waters, was the sphere of Ea, a watery deity. Later he overcame Apsu, the Abyss of Sweet Water, and built his shrine on Apsu himself. Ea was the creator of the *form* of humankind.

As soon as these three gods were begotten, and others, not mentioned by name, had come into being, they formed a confraternity of the light gods and began to map out their ways. That is to say, they began to create order out of chaos. As the gods were also associated with the stars, their "ways" were represented by the course of the planets in the heavens, and the realms over which they ruled were doubtless thought of as actual places in the sky, corresponding to heaven, earth and the watery underworld. But gradually, the Way of the Gods came to have a spiritual or psychological significance as well. By the time we come to the Chaldean Oracles or Mysteries, the spheres of the gods signified pretty much what we understand now as the astrological meaning of the planets and the zodiacal houses; that is, they represent psychological powers having a fateful effect.

This ordering activity of the gods went on for some time. There was a good deal of discussion, perhaps also of dissension, among them, in the delimiting of their ways. They had difficulty establishing their new order in regions which had earlier belonged to the chaos of Apsu and Tiamat. This is understandable enough; we, too, know what conflict and confusion can arise, what turmoil can be created in the deep unconscious when, through a gradual increase of consciousness, we seek to establish order in that great and uncharted realm that, to us, is the collective unconscious. To the Babylonians, this realm was also the great unknown, the unknowable abyss of waters, vast as the heavens above them and as untamable as the deeps beneath.

The story continues:

> The confraternity of the gods was established.
> They troubled Tiamat . . .
> Indeed they upset Tiamat's belly,
> By song in the midst of the divine abode.[38]

Apparently they sought to create order by singing it into being. Perhaps, also, they used song to control the unconscious and the demons of disorder, much as David exorcised Saul's madness by music. (1 Sam. 16:17-23) Music and rhythm produce order; so, for instance, a drum beat is an instinctive act of ordering that marks out time, as a limitation on timelessness, the chaos of mere existence. But Tiamat, embodiment of passionate emotion, did not want to be brought under the control of order. The songs of the gods upset her belly, we are told. But the gods continued to sing, and, while their song was as music to their own ears, it made a very different impression on the untamable and chaotic pair:

> Apsu (the watery abyss) could not diminish their brawl
> And Tiamat was silent . . .
> Their deeds displeased her . . .
> Their way was not good . . .

That is, their way was not good in Tiamat's eyes, for obviously, if the gods could establish a new order, she and Apsu would find their realm diminished by the amount that the gods brought into the new regime. They would be injured.

> At that time Apsu, the progenitor of the great gods,

---

[38] For this and subsequent passages from the Babylonian legend, see ibid., pp. 36ff.

> Shouted out and summoned Mummu, the steward of his house, saying
> ". . . Come, to Tiamat we will go."
> They went, they lay down (on a couch) facing Tiamat.
> They took counsel together about the gods (their children).
> Apsu took up his word and said,
> To Tiamat, the holy one . . .
> "Their 'way' has been vexatious to me.
> By day I find no peace, by night I have no rest.
> Verily I will make an end of them. I will have their 'way' scattered.
> Let there be silence established; lo, then we shall rest."
> Tiamat on hearing this
> Was stirred up to wrath and shrieked to her husband,
>   [because he proposed to kill the gods, her children]
> She cried grievously, she raged all alone,
> Her feelings were outraged.
> "What? Shall we destroy that which we have made?
> Let their 'way' be made difficult, but let us proceed in kindliness."

Here is a delightful touch of the feminine "way": we will frustrate them, but we will do it with kindness!

Apparently Apsu himself felt quite frustrated by this feminine counsel, for next he took counsel with his own masculine "way"—Mummu, the Word:

> Mummu answered and gave counsel unto Apsu.
> The counsel of Mummu was . . . unfavorable (to the gods).

He speaks of their troubled way. It is now no longer the troubling way; thus does the sophistry of masculine logic throw discredit on the opponent, for, if the way is a "troubled" one, it should obviously be abolished.

Mummu goes on:

> "Father, destroy the troubled 'way.'
> Then verily by day thou shalt find peace, (and) by night thou shalt have rest."
> Apsu heard him, his face grew bright,
> For that he was planning evil against the gods, his children.
> Mummu embraced his neck,
> Sat on his knee, he kissed him.

Evidently Apsu was very pleased with himself. He had consulted with Mummu and had found an impersonal justification for what he wanted to do: "the way is troubled." Meantime, he treated Mummu almost like a familiar spirit. He took counsel with him and embraced him, nursed him on his knee and kissed him. This picture of the god with his familiar spirit is rather a common one; it recalls an English dialect phrase, "to sit by your mommets," or "to be by your mommets." A mommet is a puppet or doll, and the phrase means to go apart with your invisible puppet, your alter ego, and brood over the situation—a tenuous remnant of the idea of taking counsel with its intelligence.

Actually, such a familiar spirit is part of the psyche, but, because it is not yet conscious, it functions autonomously. In this way Apsu took counsel with Mummu, his intelligence, for, in archaic times, thinking was not as yet a conscious function, but instead was personified and projected as an autonomous part-personality. In active imagination, we try to relate to just such split-off parts of our own psyches, in this way bringing them up to consciousness. For if they remain unconscious and we take no heed of them, our decisions will be one-sided—they will lack balance and will not hold firm when faced with the difficulties reality presents.

And now we are told of the trouble that followed this meeting of Apsu with Mummu, for the news of it spread and, the text continues,

> Whatever they planned in the assembly
> Was repeated to the gods their eldest sons.
> The gods, when they heard it, wandered about . . .
> They took to silence, sat in stillness.

The gods were evidently very much disturbed by Apsu's plan to destroy them, for we are told that Ea, the lord of the underworld and of the waters, who was a prudent god endowed with understanding, searched out the weakness of Apsu and Mummu and proceeded to make a "form" or image of them and set it up. Then, as the text says:

> He invented for it an exceedingly holy incantation,
> Repeated it, and set it (the "form") in the water,
> Emitted sleep upon it: it was lying in a corner.

This, of course, is common magical practice. Ea made an effigy of Apsu and Mummu, a magic procedure that was even stronger than invoking their names. Then he recited an incantation over it, so that those whom it imaged—Apsu and Mummu—should sleep and be helpless in his hands. In a similar way, a voodoo doctor makes an image of his enemy in wax, then melts the wax so that the enemy shall "dwine away." In psychological practice, to make an image would be tantamount to making a clear picture of the power, or inner influence, that is confronting one's conscious attitude, for instance by meditation, by reflection or by drawing. These are all ways of naming that aspect of the unconscious that is disturbing one's mental health. It becomes real, almost concrete, so that one knows just what it is that cries out for attention.

Ea's intelligence is shown in the invention of this piece of magic, and in his ability to make a sufficiently holy or "numinous" incantation to enchant the first great god himself. Difficult as this task was, he was apparently successful, for the text continues:

> (So) he caused Apsu to lie down, and sleep was emitted.
> [Apsu acted exactly as the image had acted.]
> Mummu's manly parts were cut off in a whirl.
> [Perhaps a whirl of water, a whirlpool.]

Ea's first act was to maim the god's intelligence or render it impotent.

> He (Ea) loosened his (Mummu's) joints, tore off his cap,
> Removed his light, made misery his lot.
> He overcame him, and slew Apsu,
> He bound Mummu and smashed his skull.

It is interesting to note that although the battle was against Apsu and, indeed, he was slain in the combat, yet the actual assault is on Mummu. It is he who is castrated, who loses his power, whose joints are loosened, meaning perhaps that Apsu's ideas were no longer well articulated or consecutive. Then his cap was torn off; that is, the covering of his head, symbol of his dignity and self-control, was wrested from him, and his "light" was removed, probably meaning that his eyes were put out so that his intelligence was darkened. With this, he was completely overcome. Apparently this conquest of Mummu rendered Apsu entirely helpless, for it is stated here that Ea slew Apsu at this point, without a struggle. Mummu, however, was not slain. He was bound and his skull was smashed, which would surely have finished a lesser being, but Mummu survived to be enslaved by Ea.

The story thus far has told how, through endless eons, the gods came into being and began to establish order in the chaos. But the new order they sought to create troubled the ancient gods. In particular, their clamor disturbed Apsu. If we translate this into psychological terms, it would mean that what had been the natural condition, the unconscious functioning of life, had been disturbed by the emergence of consciousness, with the need to order things in relation to an ego, a definite point in the welter of waters. Or, to put it a little differently, the named gods, personifications of man's god-like capacity for consciousness, attempted to order the chaos. They were unable to do so because forces that still determined the fates were too strong.

Correspondingly, humanity tries to order the chaos of the world without, and the chaotic unconscious within, by conscious functions, forgetting that the powers of the unconscious determine our fate, until the dragons of the unconscious have been overcome by a truly heroic struggle. But, as the gods struggled to establish ways of order, the chaos (the unconscious) was troubled—especially it was disturbed by the speech of the gods, which established councils, laws and conventions. For, if the young gods could learn to work together, the powers of the old chaotic gods would be in much greater jeopardy.

The ordering power of speech—that is, of understanding—plays a prominent part in the Biblical story of the building of the Tower of Babel, where it is said that "the whole earth was of one language, and of one speech." (Gen. 11:1) This was the situation after the Flood, when the descendants of Noah were beginning to increase in number.

> And it came to pass, as they journeyed from the east, that they found a plain in the land of Shinar; and they dwelt there.
>
> And they said to one another, Go to, let us make brick, and burn them thoroughly. And they had brick for stone, and slime had they for mortar.
>
> And they said, Go to, let us build us a city and a tower, whose top may reach unto heaven; and let us make us a name, lest we be scattered abroad upon the face of the whole earth.
>
> And the Lord came down to see the city and the tower, which the children of men builded.
>
> And the Lord said, Behold, the people is one, and they have all one language; and this they begin to do: and now nothing will be restrained from them, which they have imagined to do.
>
> Go to, let us go down, and there confound their language, that they may not understand one another's speech.
>
> So the Lord scattered them abroad from thence upon the face of all the earth: and they left off to build the city. (Gen. 11:2-8)

One of the effects of the descent of the Spirit at Pentecost was that the polyglot crowd gathered at Jerusalem heard the speech of the apostles each "in his own language." (Acts 2:6) It seems as though, when the Spirit comes to reside in each individual, the divisive effect of Yahweh's action is reversed. Before the incarnation and the indwelling of the Spirit became possible, the objective of the God of the Old Testament was to keep humanity weak and divided, for fear they might usurp the prerogatives of God. After the mission of Christ the objective was changed to make us individually whole and united together: "There shall be one shepherd and one flock."

In analysis, when dealing with a conflict in the psyche, it is most important that the individual should be able to understand what each part is trying to say. Someone in serious conflict is greatly helped by clearly articulating the conflicting urgencies that are threatening fragmentation. The analysand must try to find a language that the analyst can understand. A common language makes a deep bond, and if a person is fairly well balanced typologically,[39] and has been able to establish some understanding between the conflicting inner elements, the threat from the unconscious can be met with much greater hope of success. If the person has only one good function, thinking for instance, amenable to conscious will, chances of success are pretty slim; with two good functions chances are better; and with three—which, until the definitive fight has been won, is probably the most one can hope for—one may indeed succeed. The first prize of victory will be the cooperation of the fourth function.

In the myth, Apsu, who had attempted to stop the forward movement of the gods, his sons, was overcome as a result of this first campaign, and from his body the sacred places were made. This indicates that the unconscious, in its male form, was in some way apprehended, caught and contained in the concepts and symbols of religion. The myth goes on to describe how all this was accomplished. Ea took up his abode in the shrine, which he built upon the conquered body of Apsu, and called the shrine "The Apsu." There, in a sacred well, his son Marduk was born. We are told that when

> ... his father that begot him looked at him,
> His heart rejoiced and was glad, was filled with joy.
> He equipped him and added unto him the double form of a god
> So that he was exceedingly tall, exceeding them all a little.

At this point, the poem was apparently enacted in the ritual, for someone, perhaps a chorus, calls out: "Whose son? Whose son?" and is answered: "The Sun-god's son, the son of the gods cloaked in bright glory, he (illumines) the shrine of the gods."

And so the hero, who was destined to carry forward the evolution of consciousness, was born. His birth was acclaimed by all the gods, named and unnamed, as though they had a premonition of the significant role he was to play.

Marduk fighting Tiamat (Assyrian cylinder seal)

---

[39] See *Psychological Types,* CW 6, pars. 899f., 983ff.

3
The Fate of the Maternal Chaos
and Her Son-Husband

Before the birth of Marduk, there had been no mention of any feminine agency, except for Tiamat herself. Each generation of gods had consisted of male beings only. However, it seems that the participation of a feminine element was necessary for the creation of a hero destined to be the forerunner of human consciousness. And so we are told that Marduk was born in the well, which has a feminine connotation. It is like a womb. But this well also represented the Abyss of Apsu, so that Marduk, while being the child of Ea, was also, in a certain sense, the son of Apsu.

This double fatherhood corresponds to the condition of our human psyche. It is a theme frequently encountered in myths and fairy tales, where the hero is the child of ordinary human beings, but also the child of a god. Christian dogma is based on the same archetype, for Jesus was the son of Joseph the carpenter, but also the son of God. In fairy tales the hero is the child of peasants, or is perhaps fostered by them, while his real parents are often of royal status. Many children have fantasies that correspond to this myth, imagining themselves to be foundlings while their real parents are a king and queen. And in the grown-up fantasies of reincarnation, in the "remembered" former lives, individuals almost always claim to have been very important people.

The double parenthood, as Jung points out,[40] is enacted in our own day by the appointment of a godfather and godmother for each child received into the Christian Church at baptism. The godparents are the representatives of the deity, and it is their duty to teach the child about its divine heritage. For while we are each the children of our human parents, we are also children of God. In psychological language, we would say that the ego is the child of the human, or conscious, part of the psyche, while the Self is the child of the objective psyche, which is not personal but transcendent. For the Self is both immanent and transcendent. On one side it is related to the ego, and on the other to a not-personal aspect of the psyche of unknown dimensions and potency.

To return to our story, Ea was delighted to have a son and he equipped him with extraordinary powers, greater than any other god possessed. But apparently

---

[40] [See, for instance, "Concerning the Archetypes, with Special Reference to the Anima Concept," *The Archetypes and the Collective Unconscious*, CW 9i, par. 140.—Ed.]

the gods did not relish having Marduk made superior to themselves and they became very jealous. If we take Marduk to represent the emerging consciousness of man, this would imply that the new-born psychic factor of consciousness threatens the unrestrained activity of the gods, who of course represent the instinctive drives of the psyche. This fact is quite obvious in the case of the Greek gods, where Ares represents the martial spirit, Aphrodite stands for sensuality, Eros for love, and so on.

As one begins to develop a sense of self and to differentiate the "I" from the "not-I," one seizes a little of the power of the gods. The ego threatens their untrammeled sway. For the ego has a certain ability to choose, or, to put it another way, the ego can know its objective and has the will power to pursue it, and this is beyond the gods.

An illustration may make this clearer, for a situation comparable to the struggle between Marduk and the gods may occur when the emerging ego comes into conflict with unconscious psychic elements. The adolescent, for instance, almost proverbially takes the liberty of drowsing long after he has been called in the morning. His unconscious desire for sleep, represented by the dragon of sloth, will not yield to the call of duty conveyed by his mother's voice, and until this dragon has been overcome he will continue to indulge his desirousness. He simply does not get up. But then it is the mother who has the conflict, and that on two counts: her annoyance that the boy won't get up while breakfast is getting cold, and her anxiety lest he be late for school. The boy simply allows her to carry the responsibility for his adaptation to reality. It is a very difficult problem. If she goes on calling him while he remains stubbornly under the bedclothes, she will eventually try to force him to obey, then they will both be angry at each other. If she lets him sleep and take the consequences of being late for school, sooner or later the school will blame her!

Of course, adolescence is far too late for this problem to be confronted. It should have been met over and over again during childhood. But not until the youth realizes that the obligation to perform his task is his very own does he begin to experience all the obstinacy of the conflict within himself. Then by grappling with his own laziness, he takes a definite step in overcoming his dependence on the mother. But this action may stir up trouble in the unconscious. The unconscious may simply refuse to cooperate, just as the gods were definitely hostile to Marduk, on account of his superiority to them.

Anu, Marduk's grandfather, came to the rescue of his grandson. He "begot the four winds," we are told, with which to disperse the enemy gods. But this action had an unforeseen effect, for it stirred up Tiamat. That is to say, the unconscious in its feminine aspect became enraged. In psychological language, the most archaic aspect of the anima was aroused and created a fuss.

This situation would have an effect in real life something like this: when our youth tries to assume the responsibility of getting to school, or later to work, he finds himself beset by all the arguments of the anima—that old female who does not want to be consciously responsible. These arguments express themselves in rationalizations, such as that it won't do any harm to take "just five minutes more." The boy tries to deal with this regressive impulse by reason, perhaps, or by calling on his prestige, or by will power or the fear of punishment; that is, attempting in a masculine way to protect his hero-attempt from being undermined by his autoerotic sloth. But when it looks as if this approach of the conscious ego may be successful and he really will have to get out into the cold, an emotional reaction is usually stirred up. Something in him just won't cooperate. Perhaps he gets mad at the obligation to conform, or is sullen and sulky because he has to get up when some other fellow can stay in bed. Eventually he does get up, but by this time he is in such a rage that his clothes all frustrate him and he arrives for breakfast late and in a vile temper. This is the sort of thing that is meant by Tiamat's being disturbed. It is a very minor instance of this problem. In larger matters the disturbance may be correspondingly magnified.

"Tiamat was stirred up . . . by day and night," we are told. Here there is a gap in the text, but presumably she made many loud complaints. On a former occasion, when she had been disturbed by the way of the gods, she had shrieked aloud, and so we may suppose she was no less unrestrained now. For the text relates that the gods of her retinue bore her tumult in misery, until they could bear it no longer, and then "their bellies planned evil." Their thoughts were not in their heads, but in their bellies, the seat of unconscious passion. To this day many primitive peoples do not place the seat of thought in the head. Some put it in the abdomen, others in the chest. It is a late development to think in the head. Even in current times, an emotional situation we ought to consider carefully may get so out of hand that the disturbance in our stomach may speak hot words which we had not intended to say at all.

Now Tiamat had taken no part in the struggle with Ea, though it was largely on account of her disturbance that Apsu interfered with the gods and the new "ways" they wanted to establish. And so the unnamed dark gods, servants of the first great potencies, went to Tiamat and reproached her for her attitude, saying,

> When they slew Apsu, thy spouse,
> Thou wast not marching at his side, but didst sit weeping.

This reminder so stirred up Tiamat that she decided to make war on the gods of light who formed the retinue of Anu, whose winds had disturbed her peace.

When Apsu, the male potency, had been disturbed by the ways of the gods, he had not taken direct action against them, but had contented himself with talk and plans. And it was when these plans came to the ears of the gods that they took action and killed Apsu, before he had made any move at all, but was still taking counsel with Mummu, his intelligence.

Tiamat, being female, wasted no time on words. She got things moving at once. First she created certain demons to reinforce her own retinue of dark gods, and then she called on her half-sister to help her. It is by no means unusual for a goddess to have a half-sister who represents the dark or underworld aspect of the feminine principle, connected with the symbolism of the moon and its phases, now light, now dark. The dark half-sister usually lives in the underworld. Sometimes she is hostile, at others she wields powers of magic and healing. So, for instance, Inanna-Ishtar, Sumerian Goddess of Heaven and Earth, had a half-sister, Ereshkigal, who was queen of the underworld.[41] Isis of Egyptian mythology is sometimes pictured as white and sometimes as black, and in some Christian churches there are shrines to the Black Virgin, who has power over the forces of disease, madness, famine and so on.

The half-sister of Tiamat was said to fashion all things. She must represent that aspect of the unconscious that brings forth all possible shapes, the horrid phantoms of nightmare, the fantasies of the insane, the uncanny terrors of the dark, for we are told that "she spawned huge serpents, grim monstrous serpents, arrayed in terror," and other horrors. Then, not content with having created these terrible creatures, she proceeded to disguise them as creatures of the light.

This is a maneuver we are all familiar with in our encounters with the unconscious. Who has not found, in a time of serious conflict, that what seems to be good may well have an evil effect, or that some action or attitude that we would ordinarily condemn as thoroughly black begins to appear as the only right way? The unconscious can cause such confusion between what is right and what is evil that the ego can easily be led astray. The dilemma is of such a nature that there is no clearly marked right, no solution that is only good when judged by the ordinary canons of right and wrong. Thus the ego cannot decide on the basis of any general standard. Only a judgment based on an individual way—that is, one in which the Self as well as ego-consciousness takes part—can resolve the insoluble conflict. But this, at the time of our myth, was as yet not possible; the gods were too powerful.

As soon as her half-sister had completed her preparations, Tiamat created the

---

[41] [For a detailed psychological commentary on Inanna-Ishtar and Ereshkigal, see Sylvia Brinton Perera, *Descent to the Goddess: A Way of Initiation for Women.*—Ed.]

eleven constellations of the zodiac. (The twelfth constellation was only added much later.) One of these was represented by Tiamat's own son, Kingu, whom she took as spouse. She entrusted the leadership of the demons to him and called him her *"only*-spouse." Apparently she had entirely forgotten Apsu and her connection with him. The primitive mother goddesses always have this kind of promiscuity. They live in accordance with the emotion of the moment—nothing else exists for them. So long as they are emotionally involved they are faithful, but no sooner has their passion cooled than they entirely forget the object of their devotion and become involved with the next person who attracts their attention. This is quite characteristic of the way in which unconscious emotionality acts, too. The intensity of the moment represents the supreme value. The individual caught up in such an emotional storm either submits to the instinctive drive surging up from the unconscious—that is to say, gives in to Tiamat—or enlists every conscious resource so as not to be swept away. This would involve a struggle, however, that only the hero can hope to survive.

I think much of the promiscuity of modern times is due to a lack of understanding of the values concerned. During the Victorian culture instincts were so repressed and ego and intellect so highly valued, that the energies of the unconscious, like Tiamat, rebelled. Now we need a new savior, a hero who can perhaps win a battle against them and retrieve their energies for the purposes of life. Certainly, to go back to the old moral attitudes, toward sex for instance, or filial obedience, will not solve the problem. New wine must be put into new bottles, and there is no doubt that the rebellion against the old order is fermenting a new wine that is decidedly heady.

Tiamat's son, Kingu, is probably an early form of Tammuz, who, like Kingu, was also both son and spouse of his mother, Ishtar. This is an archetypal theme that Freud has made familiar to everyone with his emphasis on the Oedipus complex. But while there the emphasis falls on the son's longing for a return to the womb, here the emphasis is on the mother's need to keep her son with her, to satisfy her emotional needs and also to assist in her struggle against change.

This dual relation between the mother goddess and the masculine partner, who is both son and spouse, is characteristic of the stories of the dying and resurrecting gods. Kingu plays this part in our myth, and later he fulfilled another element of the mythologem for he was sacrificed in order that man might be created. Again we have analogies to the Christian dogma, which states that when Mary was assumed into heaven she entered at once into the nuptial chamber. Now, of course, this does not imply that Mary is Tiamat, or that Christ and Kingu are identical. But it does mean that the archetypal imagery repeated itself over and over on many levels. The law that governs the unfolding of the most primitive conception of deity is the same law that operates when we come to a more spiritual understanding of the divine factors that rule inner life. So when we read this ancient myth, we can find in it an understanding of the eternal forces that are at work in the world today, just as they were in ancient Babylon.

Kingu, then, was one of the dying gods who belong to the underworld. Also, true to the mythologem, he was raised up by Tiamat to become the moon. This too is typical of such gods. Osiris, in Egyptian mythology, was spouse of his sister-mother Isis, and after his death he became lord and judge of the underworld, but he also shared with his mother the realm of the moon. Tiamat gave the Tablet of Destinies, which belonged to her, into Kingu's care. This is a reference to the fate-determining power often ascribed to the moon. By this action Tiamat gave up some of her despotic power to Kingu. For in order to be able to combat the way of the upper gods it was imperative that she submit to a certain order herself. She had to renounce her authority, her whim, as sole determinant of the fate of the universe. Untrammeled emotion could no longer rule. So we see that the gods of light gained a concession from the female realm.

Tiamat handed the determination of the fates over to Kingu, who, as moon, followed a set course in the heavens and was not merely the expression of chaos. It is true that the moon does not follow the same laws as the other heavenly bodies, but wanders over the heavens in what, to the ancients, must have seemed like a self-willed and arbitrary fashion. But even so, Kingu's way was much more comprehensible than the ways of Tiamat. So in fighting the new order of the gods, Tiamat had succumbed already in some measure to its influence. She established an order herself, a feminine way.

One might remark in passing that this is a phenomenon that can also be observed in our own psychological battles against the overwhelming power of the unconscious. As soon as we begin to pay attention to it, the chaos within the unconscious begins to be resolved. Powerful and menacing it may still be, but the dreams and fantasies that arise from it tend to become more ordered and comprehensible.

The text goes on to describe the powers that Tiamat gave to Kingu for the coming struggle. "She gave him the Tablet of Destinies" (which had belonged to her—that is, to the feminine unconscious—from the beginning). Then she sent him forth to destroy the gods and the order they had begun to establish.

Here the first tablet ends, as Rogers tells us, "in chaos and wild threats and inhuman passions, and strange monsters and mighty forces of disorder."[42] The male aspect of the wild watery chaos had been overcome by the gods and made

---

[42] Rogers, *The Religion of Babylonia and Assyria,* p. 118.

into their sacred abode, *The* Apsu, and the gods—that is, the celestial gods—
were engaged in establishing their "way." But now the female aspect of primal
chaos, the dark region of emotions, took up the fight against order. Tiamat was
thoroughly aroused and had already created a seemingly invincible army to put
the gods to rout.

And so the second tablet opens with Tiamat and her hosts arrayed for battle.
She sent a challenge to the gods notifying them that this time she intended to
destroy them. From here on the form of the text suggests that the ritual was enacted instead of being merely read.[43]

> When Anshar [father of Anu and grandfather of Ea] heard that Tiamat
>   was stirring mightily,
> . . . he bit his lips
> . . . his mind was not at peace.

He addressed Ea and said:

> "Thou hast slain Mummu and Apsu
> But Tiamat hath exalted Kingu—where is the one who can meet her?"

Here there is a long gap in the text, which then continues:

> Anshar spake a word unto his son (Anu):—
> ". . . this is a difficulty, my warrior . . .
> Go and stand thou in the presence of Tiamat,
> That her spirit (be quieted), her heart softened.
> But should she not hearken unto thy word,
> Speak thou our (incantation) unto her so that she may be abated."

The use of the word "abated" recalls Tiamat's nature as the Ocean Chaos.
The text then goes on to tell how Anu went to Tiamat but could not prevail
against her. He turned back and went in terror to his father, Anshar. At this,

> Anshar was distressed, he looked down upon the ground,
> He was silent; towards Ea he lifted up his head.

But apparently Ea was unwilling to accept the task, and the gods said:

> "Nowhere is there a god who will attack Tiamat.
> He would not escape from Tiamat's presence with his life."
> The Lord Anshar, the Father of the gods (rose) majestically,
> He reflected in his heart, he addressed the gods (saying)
> "He whose (strength) is mighty (shall be) an avenger for (us)
> . . . Marduk the Hero."

---

[43] Smith, *Babylonian Legends,* pp. 44ff.

Then they called to Marduk and asked him whether he would undertake the task. Tiamat's preparations were simply appalling to the light gods, and apparently not less so to the Babylonians who recorded them, for there are four different descriptions of them on the first three tablets.

However, Marduk was not overwhelmed by fear on hearing of Tiamat's strength, for we are told:

> The Lord (Marduk) rejoiced at the word of his father,
> He approached and took up his place before Anshar.
> Anshar looked upon him and his heart was filled with gladness.
> He (*i.e.*, Anshar) kissed his (Marduk's) lips, and his (Anshar's) fear
>   was removed. (Then Marduk said) . . .
> "I will go, I will cause to take place all that is in thy heart."

Anshar then mapped out a course of action for Marduk, who rejoiced at the mission he was given, but made certain conditions. He said:

> "O Lord of the gods, Fate of the Great Gods,
> If I am to be your avenger
> To slay Tiamat and bestow life upon you,
> Summon a meeting, proclaim and magnify my position . . .
> Let me determine destinies . . . even as ye do."

And so Marduk, who is a hero because he is a son of the gods, is yet much nearer to human consciousness than the older gods, and here he made a very good bargain for himself. If he overcame Tiamat, then he would be the equal of the greatest gods, he would even surpass them. This surely foretells the next stage of consciousness, when man, by his developed conscious ego, became like unto a god, harnessing the forces of nature and making her serve his purpose—at least for a season.

The story goes on to tell how Anshar called all the gods together to bestow powers on Marduk, for even the greatest god could not bestow these powers by his own authority, since there was as yet no conception of a supreme deity as we know it. When the gods arrived, Anshar gave them a big feast and made them all a little drunk so that they should fall in with his wishes.

> They ate bread, they mixed (wine),
> The taste of the sweet drink changed their cares.
> Through drinking strong liquor their bodies were filled to overflowing,
> They made much merry music . . .
> They issued the decree for Marduk as their avenger.

They gave him all that he had asked and more. And here there follows a very strange incident, the description of a piece of mimetic magic. Apparently the gods were not absolutely sure that the powers they had conferred upon Marduk would be sufficient to ensure his victory in the epic struggle that was to take place, for had not both Anu and Ea already tried to confront the all-powerful mother, and each retreated abashed and confounded by the terror her very presence inspired? And so they arranged a test:

> They had a cloak set in their midst,
> They addressed the god Marduk their first-born (saying):
> "Thou, Lord, shalt hold the foremost position among the gods.
> Decree thou the throwing down and the building up, and it shall come to pass.
> Speak but the word, and the cloak shall be no more,
> Speak a second time and the cloak shall be intact."

The garment that the gods set up represented the vault of the sky and the curve of the nether seas conceived as one whole round. This figure of the unbroken circle of primeval chaos corresponds to the uroboros before the opposites came into being. The waters above the firmament were not as yet divided from the waters below. Such was Mother Tiamat. In Egyptian art, the corresponding figure, Nut, is represented as an oval, egg-shaped form, studded with stars. These stars correspond to the demons that Tiamat created and made into the constellations. In the coming struggle Marduk was to split apart the lower half of this oval from its upper half by blowing the wind into Tiamat's belly—that is, he created the firmament of air that, according to Genesis, separates the waters that are above from the waters that are below. And eventually Marduk set up new gods to rule the heavens.

But first he had to prove his competence. If he could enchant the garment so it split into two pieces and then reconstruct it by magic, he would be able to deal with Tiamat in a similar way. Indeed, in the world of magic Tiamat would already have been defeated by the act of enchanting the garment. For this is the way of magical thought. There was a previous example of this kind of magic in our text, when Ea made an image of Apsu and Mummu and put it to sleep in a corner, with the result that the god and his intelligence also went to sleep, being hypnotized by Ea's magic. Now a similar piece of magic is to be performed, but the experiment is carried a step further, for the gods demand a demonstration. Marduk must show his power by making the cloak actually disappear and then reappear at his command.

To us this seems like a fantastic and unreal story, but actually it isn't. It is a mythical expression of a psychological truth. If, for instance, a person is confronted by some task, some ordeal that seems impossibly difficult, he or she may perhaps refuse it, realizing that it would require an impossible measure of courage, wisdom or strength. Or one may go away alone and confront the problem in solitude, call on a greater power for help, perhaps by prayer and meditation, or by introversion, which is not so very different. In either case one submits to this higher power in whose service he or she can dare the dangers. It is through this renunciation of personal ego-will that the hero really wins victory—not only over self, but also a victory in the outer world. For if this is the attitude, whether things go as hoped or not, they are not distorted by willful intervention. A classic example of this kind of inner "magic" is found in the relations between Gethsemane, Calvary and the empty tomb.

And so Marduk was challenged to prove his competence. The tension and anxiety among the gods as they waited for the outcome is evidenced by their joy and relief at its success:

> Marduk spoke the word, the cloak was no more,
> He spoke a second time, the cloak reappeared.
> When the gods his fathers saw the issue of the utterance of his mouth
> They rejoiced and adored (him, saying), "Marduk is King . . .
> Go, cut off the life of Tiamat.
> Let the wind carry her blood into the depth (under the earth)."

Then follows the story of the battle of the hero against the enraged primal Mother and all her destructive powers, who had gathered together to overthrow her insolent opponent. Marduk immediately set to work to arm himself:

> The gods, his fathers, issued the decree for the god Bel. [Bel means Lord.]
> They set him on the road which leadeth to peace and obedience.

First they took the lightning and set it in front of his face. This was the gift of his grandfather, Anu. It represents the ability to penetrate the darkness of the chthonic abyss by the power of light, that is, of understanding. Next he called the winds of the four quarters to surround his chariot. These would be his normal guards and were the contribution of Enlil, the earth god, who was also Lord of Winds. In addition, he summoned three other winds, "the foul wind," "the storm" and "the parching blast." These are the winds of the desert where the reign of chaos was still unconquered. So already, probably as the first result of his magic act, Marduk could command the powers of the unordered regions and turn them against the chaos of Mother Tiamat. And lastly he made a great net in which he planned to encompass her so that she could not escape, for he realized that one of the greatest difficulties he would encounter in trying to overcome chaos, the vasty deep, would be to capture it. The same difficulty confronts us when we attempt to deal with the collective unconscious. It ever eludes us and reappears just out of reach.

Having made his preparations, Marduk set out:

> He took a direct path, he hastened on his journey.
> He set his face towards the place of Tiamat.

Marduk's attitude of assurance is very different from the anxiety and hesitation Anu and Ea had shown, but they had failed to make adequate preparations for the cosmic struggle. Marduk avoided this mistake, for, in addition to having made careful preparations, he had sought and obtained the support of the gods:

> Then the gods drag him along,
> The gods, his fathers, drag him, the gods drag him along.

The reiteration of the fact that the gods drag the chariot, and the use of the present tense, suggest that this part of the ritual poem was indeed enacted. The text continues:

> The Lord approached, and looked upon the middle of Tiamat.

Sidney Smith points out that in a later tablet Marduk is said to have "entered into the middle of Tiamat," where Kingu had taken up his position.[44] "Middle" could be either belly or womb, recalling a drawing of the Egyptian goddess, Nut, who corresponds to Tiamat, in which she is shown as a belly containing a god who is curled in the embryonic position. So Kingu is like an embryo within Tiamat's belly.

To go on with the story:

> He searches out the weakness of Kingu, her husband.
> Marduk looks, Kingu staggers in his gait. [This is the "look" of magic
>   power, comparable to the evil eye.]
> His (Kingu's) will was destroyed, his motion was paralyzed.
> And the gods his helpers who were marching by his side
> Saw their chief and their sight was troubled.
> Tiamat (shrieked but) did not turn her head.
> With lips full of (rebellious words) she maintained her stubbornness,
> (Saying), ". . . thou has come as the Lord of the gods, (forsooth),
> They have gathered together from their own places in thy place."
> The Lord (*i.e.,* Marduk) raised up the wind-storm, his mighty weapon,
> (Against) Tiamat, who was furious, he sent it, (saying):
> "(Thou hast made thyself) mighty, thou art puffed up on high,
> Thy heart (hath stirred thee up) to invoke battle . . .
> Let now thy troops gird themselves up, let them bind on their weapons.
> Stand up! Thou and I, let us to the fight!"

---

[44] Ibid., p. 23.

> On hearing these words Tiamat
> Became like a mad thing, her senses became distraught.
> Tiamat uttered shrill cries furiously,
> Her lower limbs trembled from the base in rhythm,
> She recalled an incantation, she pronounced her spell.

So Tiamat brought *her* magic against Marduk's. This was a fateful moment, fraught with dire possibilities. And our own fight against the engulfing power of the unconscious is just as fateful. For as soon as we challenge the supremacy of the unconscious it becomes disturbed and threatening; its chaotic character becomes more marked, just as Tiamat "became like a mad thing." Then the unconscious begins to cast a spell upon us: either we become enchanted by the fearsome spectacles that unfold themselves in our dreams and fantasies, so that even the world around us may seem bewitched, or we are overwhelmed with drowsiness as though, as the text puts it, a spell of deep sleep has "been emitted upon us"; or perhaps we become so bewildered and distraught that we no longer know who we are nor what we are doing.

For example, during the course of analysis a woman in her late thirties dreamed that she was walking on a wide sandy beach on a sunny day:

> Down near the water, quite a distance from her, there was a group of children playing at the water's edge. Behind a sand bank she came to a pool left by the tide and as she was walking through it she saw a lump of jet. She stooped and picked it up, feeling it to be a treasure in the form of the *nigredo,* of which the alchemists tell. But immediately a cold wind blew over the scene. The children left their play and hurried to find shelter, for wracks of cloud began to race up the sky. She too turned to go in, but found herself in quicksand, buffeted by a wind of increasing violence, rising to gale proportions, while rain and hail beat down upon her. She lost her sense of direction and for a time feared she would be engulfed, but she persisted in her struggle, holding on tightly to the precious black jewel. As the dream ended she was nearing the safety of the sea wall.

The treasure she had seized at such risk was a symbol of the Self, and because the archetypal image of the parents had not suffered severe or pathological injury in her case, she was able to reach safety without relinquishing it. But if the parents have not carried the parental image satisfactorily, having, perhaps, presented to their child a picture of selfishness and discord, the archetypal image will have suffered serious damage. Even in those cases where the child was cared for on the material side, if no spiritual values were honored then the problem of rescuing the treasure from the unconscious may be much more difficult than for those persons in whose childhood homes these values were taught. Such a person may dream of the treasure, as this woman did, but when the dreamer tries to retrieve it, the whole scene may turn negative. Then the dreamer may fall into a nightmare of impenetrable darkness and black waters. Sometimes, before final disaster overtakes the dreamer, some religious symbol emerges. It may be only a hint, but it represents a last chance to take the right attitude. If the image of the saving archetype has been very seriously damaged, the redemptive interlude may attract hardly any attention. Only when the dream is analyzed will the dreamer become aware that salvation was offered.

In the case of the woman who found the piece of jet, her action in taking it was equivalent to the theft of a treasure. The powers of the deep were threatened, as is evidenced by the reaction of wind and water when their primordial possession was taken away. A similar situation is portrayed in the theft of the Rheingold that led eventually to the *Götterdämmerung.* The black jewel is a symbol of the Self in its original nigredo condition. Jet is fossilized carbon. It is very old and so expresses the fact that the treasure of the Self has lain hidden in the depths of the psyche from time immemorial. The woman's action corresponds to the Promethean theft of the fire of the gods, and the unconscious powers were injured by her success. This is a common occurrence in the hero's struggle, and the inevitable injury produced by the hero's act is one which appears in many versions of this mythologem.

Where the dreamer cannot endure the ordeal and possess the treasure, a much more serious problem is involved. For the injury to the archetypal image is of a different kind from that inevitably inflicted by the hero's struggle. For instance, if the experience of the actual parents has been negative, the conscious attitude of the individual will be characterized by negative feelings and resistance toward them. But this condition will be compensated in the unconscious by a particularly strong tie, which may be represented in dream images such as being haunted by a dead parent, perhaps, or being buried in the parent's grave.

Alternatively, the parent may appear in dreams in the guise of a devouring monster. In the story of Little Red Riding Hood, the wolf that ate up the kind grandmother appeared in the guise of the terrible grandmother who would devour the child too. In cases of this sort, if there has been no spiritual teaching, the situation will be all the more damaging, even if, on the conscious level, the parents have been kind. If the religion that was taught was of a stern and vindictive God, the child cannot make use of the symbols of redemption, even though they may be presented in dreams. The sacrificed Christ, for example, will seem a travesty of justice, involving the condemnation of a son by a terribly cruel father; it will never symbolize the love and devotion of a savior.

In such cases it is as if childhood, instead of being a Garden of Eden, with its paradisiacal connotations, has been a desert, and in consequence the child is separated by an impassable chasm from the world of promise, where the symbol of the Self might be found. Normally, if the child should encounter a satisfactory parent substitute, this gap may be bridged in outer life. The experience of parental care and guidance found with the substitute parent may give one an opportunity to outgrow one's dependence, which will surely be great because it rests on an unconscious compensation for the experience of the actual parents who have proved unsatisfactory.

In the adult, a similar reconstruction of the damaged image may occur in the analytic situation, where the transference of the parent imago onto the analyst provides a means by which the gap may be bridged. This usually comes about by means of religious symbols appearing in the dreams that replace the person of the analyst, and so lead the libido over into an inner or subjective realm where the person may find security. Jung gives an account of just such a development in the case of a woman he analyzed, where his own person was replaced in a dream by the image of an antique god who carried the patient in his arms and gave her a part in the eternal ritual of nature's renewal.[45] But where the archetypal image has been seriously injured and the religious symbols have been so distorted that they can no longer serve the individual's need, one wonders whether the image can ever be repaired so as to function normally.

Our epic does not portray any such pathological case; rather it represents the way mankind has followed through the ages; that is, it is the normal adventure— those who were unequal to the ordeal perished along the way and their defeat did not leave its trace on this particular mythologem.

The crucial question at this stage of Marduk's fight was whether his magic would prove to be powerful enough to overcome Tiamat's, for if not, Marduk would be repulsed as his father and grandfather had been before him. They had retreated from Tiamat before ever engaging her directly, but Marduk could not do this. He had gone so far that a decisive encounter had to be risked. So he distributed their weapons to the gods, his helpers, and then, we are told,

> Tiamat and Marduk, the envoy of the gods, rushed at one another.

So even in the excitement of the fray, it seems that Marduk remembered he was not fighting with only his own strength, nor only for his own advantage. He was the envoy of the gods. Similarly, when in our struggle against the forces of the unconscious we are obliged to challenge their baleful and magic power, this is the right attitude for us, too, to take. Like Marduk, we also are not fighting alone, nor are we seeking a victory for our personal ego. The urge to conscious-

---

[45] *Two Essays on Analytical Psychology,* CW 7, pars. 211ff.

ness, strangely enough, arises out of the unconscious itself, and in our struggle the as-yet-unknown Self that, as it were, *wishes* to become conscious, is on our side. The account continues:

> They [Tiamat and Marduk] met in close conflict, they were linked in struggle.

It was no armchair fight of theories or ideologies, but a hand-to-hand melee.

> The Lord cast his net and made it to enclose her.

Marduk was not going to let her use her greatest asset, the ability to escape and reform beyond his reach. This is a common characteristic of the battle tactics of the unconscious, for although the unborn Self "wishes" to become conscious, the unconscious as a whole resists consciousness. When one element threatens to overwhelm us with its sinister power, it may seem to be defeated at the first assault, but in reality this is only a ruse to put us off guard and to soothe us into unconsciousness again. If we do not hold fast the evil will shortly reappear, powerful as ever, though perhaps disguised in a new and strange form.

This is the theme of Herakles' encounter with Nereus, for when Herakles discovered the god who held the necessary secret and tried to wrestle with him, the god changed his shape and escaped, only to reappear in one form after another. The hero persisted and finally captured the god, obtaining the reward from him. The American Indians call this figure "Shape-Shifter." He is a manifestation of Mercurius, who to the alchemists was the first metal and father of all metals, or the first planet and father of all planets, whose characteristic is that he can disappear and reform himself again, just as mercury can be sublimated by heat, only to deposit itself once more on the glass container.

Marduk did not intend to be fooled in this way:

> [He] cast his net and made it to enclose her,
> The evil wind that had its place behind him he let out in her face.

How are we to interpret the net that Marduk made? What would it mean psychologically? In our own struggle with unconsciousness, and especially with the maternal archetype, it would mean weaving a continuous web of consciousness around the situation so that no intimations of the unconscious could escape our attention.

For instance, to go back to our adolescent who was struggling to gain his freedom from his parents—perhaps he has earned the right to take a girl out in the family car. In spite of a tiny anxiety as to whether he will have enough pocket money left to pay for extra gas, he goes ahead and then, when the tank is empty, he blandly asks the girl to pay for the gas, as though she ought to play the part of the parent who has always seen to it that these things were taken care of. Such a boy has obviously not really won his freedom from the parents. His net has a hole in it. His twinge of anxiety could have warned him to beware.

So, to make a net it is necessary to see that no hole is left where Tiamat, the mother complex, symbol of our own childish unconsciousness, can escape.

What, then, is this evil wind that Marduk let loose in Tiamat's face? Could it not be the negative affect of the son too long enclosed in the mother-world? Certainly this is the way Freudians would take it. The aggressive and negative feelings of the child in relation to the mother are encouraged by them and allowed every sort of destructive expression. An evil wind is blown out in the face of the actual personal mother. Now, while in the life of many people some experience of the negative relation to the actual mother may be necessary, and is either lived directly or, more favorably, worked out in the negative phase of the transference to the analyst, it should be borne in mind that the revolt is not primarily against the personal mother, but rather against the archetype of Mother. Even in cases where the personal mother is demanding and possessive, freedom can only be gained through the inner struggle against "Tiamat," and never by rebelling against the personal mother alone.

Indeed, the fight against the personal possessive mother never comes to an end unless Tiamat, the embodiment of unconscious instinct and emotionality, has been met. Even if the personal mother were dead, the youth would still have to struggle against her in his own psyche, while all the time remaining subject to her chaotic moods.

To go on with the story, Marduk cast his net over Tiamat and enclosed her. Then he called the evil wind from behind him and let it out in her face.

> Tiamat opened her mouth to its greatest extent,
> Marduk made the evil wind to enter her so that her lips could not unclose,
> The raging winds filled out her belly,
> Her heart was gripped, she opened wide her mouth (panting)
> Marduk shot the arrow, he split up her belly,
> He clave open her bowels, he pierced (her) heart,
> He brought her to naught and destroyed her life.
> He cast down her carcass, and took his stand upon it.

So Tiamat was overcome by this evil wind after she had been caught in the net. Surely that means that after we have captured the unconscious instinct that is the cause of our inner compulsions, our own negative reactions against this power—not, please note, our aggression and negative reactions against a human being, on whom the power of Tiamat has been projected, but our reactions against the inner bondage—then these "winds," even though they have to be designated as evil, can be used to split up the belly of Tiamat. This means to divide or analyze this inner compulsion into its opposites. For one half of Tiamat was elevated to form the dome of heaven, while the other half made the underpinning of the world—that is, one part was spiritual and the other chthonic.

It is interesting to note that in the case of the fight against Apsu, it was Mummu, his intelligence, that had to be grappled with and destroyed, while here the main struggle is with Mother Tiamat herself. Kingu, her spouse and deputy, is disposed of with very little trouble at a later time. This seems to suggest that when the assault from the unconscious is in the realm of thought, it can be met in a more impersonal, somewhat less intimate way than is the case when the problem lies in the region of the emotions. For then intelligence of the mind cannot help; intelligence of the heart is what is needed.

The story continues:

> After Marduk had slain Tiamat, the leader,
> Her retinue was scattered, her levies became fugitive,
> And the gods [or demons], her allies, who had marched at her side,
> Quaked with terror, and broke and ran
> And betook themselves to flight to save their lives.
> But they found themselves hemmed in, they could not escape.

Then Marduk confined them "in a dark place," corresponding to the idea that the demons have their dwelling place in hell; or in analytic terms we might say that Marduk dismissed them into the unconscious. So the struggle is not over!

Marduk next turned his attention to Kingu and crushed him, for he considered him of little worth, as though he were a dead god. And:

> Marduk took from him the Tablet of Destinies, which should never have been his,
> He sealed it with a seal and fastened it on his breast.

In this way Marduk took upon himself the responsibility for the destiny of the world, and as we shall see later he made suitable arrangements to safeguard this precious tablet. When the Babylonians heard these words of the ritual poem they must have realized that they had a personal responsibility for their own fate. Perhaps the more conscious among them resolved never to allow the Tablet of Destinies to fall again into the hands of Chaos and her son-husband.

Here we can see the very beginnings of personal freedom, the sense of responsibility and, too, the beginning of democracy. For tyranny starts when one person becomes possessed by the demons of Chaos (Kingu or Tiamat) and identifies, consciously or unconsciously, with the role of tyrant. That person seizes the Tablet of Destinies, as it were, and so obtains power to order the destiny of the majority, as we have seen in communist and fascist countries. But if the hero wins, then we gain the power to make our own plans and to that extent choose our fate.[46] But unfortunately the commitment to consciousness has been forgotten many times since that day, and each of those times Chaos has reigned.

This is the second time in our poem that we are told that the Babylonians recognized that humanity might play a part in the fate of the world and not remain puppets, utterly dependent on the whim of the gods. The first indication that we might have some freedom of will was hinted at on the tablet describing the function of the stars as determiners of fate. There it stated that humans might make their own plans—"the skilled for the skilled, and the fool for the fool." But in order that even this amount of freedom may be won today, each individual has to face a personal encounter with the powers of the unconscious. Those who are successful will win their own freedom, but only if they also find a means of making peace with the inner powers through an attitude corresponding to the religious devotion of the Babylonians—and then they must accept the results of their own choices. If a person is skilled, meaning wise, then the outcome will be fortunate, but a fool will always make foolish decisions. Still, even the foolish person helps to shape his or her own fate, and so cannot put all the blame, or all the credit either, onto the gods.

The poem continues:

> After he had crushed and slain his enemies . . .
> The valiant Marduk imposed strict restraint on the gods whom he had made captive.
> He turned back to Tiamat whom he had defeated,
> The Lord (Marduk) trampled on the rump of Tiamat,
> With his unsparing club he clave her skull.
> He slit open the channels of her blood.
> He caused the North Wind to carry it away to a place underground.

In this way the decree of the gods was fulfilled.

> His fathers [*i.e.,* the gods] looked on, they rejoiced, they were glad.
> They brought unto him offerings of triumph and peace.

But Marduk was not to be distracted from his still uncompleted task:

> The Lord (Marduk) paused, he examined Tiamat's carcass,
> He divided the foetus.

The foetus of Tiamat was considered to be the living germ from which the universe was constructed, and perhaps, looked at from another point of view Kingu represented this germ. So we see that when we in our turn have achieved a victory over the forces of the unconscious, our task is not yet complete. The first thing to do is to "examine the carcass"; that is, to go over the whole dis-

---

[46] See Langdon, *Semitic*, p. 314.

turbing episode, and in the relative quiet that follows such an emotional struggle to try to discover the elements that had so stirred up Tiamat. This is by no means easy to do, for such a recapitulation is all too apt to arouse her all over again, showing that she is not so dead after all. And so we hear that Marduk turned away from the triumphal offerings of the gods and continued with his work:

> He slit Tiamat open like a shell-fish into two pieces, [just as he had the cloak]
> The one half he raised up and made the heavens as a shade therewith.
> He pulled the bolt, he posted a guard,
> He ordered them not to let her water escape. [That is, the waters that
>   are above the firmament. It was also a safeguard against a deluge.]
> He crossed heaven, he contemplated the regions thereof.

Then, having reviewed the whole new world that had been gained from Tiamat's realm, he established a sacred abode, or temple, for the three named gods, in exact replica of the three realms—heaven, earth and the underworld. And so, no sooner had Marduk finished his fight and obtained the prize of victory than he set out to order chaos and control the destinies. This shows that he had already released himself in some measure from the ancient powers. It would have been natural for him to rest and feast after such a victory, but he realized that chaos is not conquered unless order is established.

This is a lesson that the Western powers learned to some extent from the experience of the First World War. When the Treaty of Versailles had been signed, the conquerors withdrew and left the conquered nations to deal with the chaos following their defeat. But this they were totally unable to do, until they reorganized themselves under a tyrant and then the evil powers of expansionism and aggression reigned once more. After the Second World War, the allies had learned some wisdom, and at least attempted to establish order and prosperity in the conquered countries. It is a truth that is applicable to personal relationships as well as international ones.

So Marduk began to divide up the territories and powers among the gods of light. That is, a masculine order was established and the old feminine way was cast out. All through the Semitic world the masculine principle was indeed held supreme. Yahweh ruled alone in heaven and claimed undivided service from the people. The ancient Dea Syria was discredited and her sanctuaries destroyed. But it was repeatedly demonstrated that she retained some power, for in any serious crisis Yahweh's chosen people turned to her again for help and comfort. On earth men, whom Yahweh had created in his own likeness, possessed the land and made the laws, while woman became a vessel, almost a slave to men. But in the course of history, that which had been despised and rejected of men was set up on high. The Son of the Mother, whose prototype was Kingu or Tammuz, made his appearance and lived his extraordinary destiny, dying that man might live, which, we shall see, also happened to Kingu.

Marduk proceeded to take possession of the realm he had won. First he established places for the gods, and as they were always inclined to quarrel he set them widely apart, giving each a starry constellation as his abode. He instructed them to mark out the months, and to Sinn, the moon, he committed the nights "to determine the day" and to measure the days by his horn and his crown. So that the days, or rather the nights, of the month were to be counted by the phases of the moon, as indeed they were right down to Roman times. A vestige of this practice remains in our own account of time, for we speak of half a month as a fortnight—not fourteen days, but fourteen nights.

In the daytime the masculine principle of intellect and conscious order rules, but at night we pass into the realm of the unconscious, where the feminine holds sway, for in mythology the moon belongs to the Mother Goddesses or to their sons. And for man this part of the twenty-four hours is ruled by the anima, his feminine soul-figure, mistress of the unconscious.

The rest of this tablet is missing, but apparently it contained an account of the discontent of the gods. When they had been established in their places in heaven, they grew tired of their isolation and perhaps of their preeminence as well—it is but an empty power if there is no one to rule over—and they began to complain that their existence was barren. There were no worshipers at their shrines, and as no one brought them offerings they were very poor.

In order to cope with this unforeseen difficulty and to satisfy the gods, Marduk devised another "cunning plan," an indication that the hero in man must be clever and creative as well as brave. He announced his intention to provide worshipers. He said that he would create man out of blood and bone:

> I will solidify blood, I will form bone.
> I will set up man, "Man" (shall be) his name.
> I will create the man "Man."
> The service of the gods shall be established, and they shall be at rest.
> I will make twofold the ways of the gods, and I will beautify (them).
> They are (now) grouped together in one place, but they shall be partitioned in two.

Man, spelled with a capital M, signifies the very essence of man, the Anthropos, as it was later called, and it is a symbol of the Self. The text states that Man was to be created with the sole purpose that he should serve the gods, so that the gods might be at rest—meaning that the forces of the unconscious within us can be satisfied, tamed, by a ritual sacrifice and by a religious attitude on the part of each individual. And it is further indicated that this service must be made by Man, again with a capital; that is, it must not be a merely perfunctory performance of the prescribed ritual made by the conscious ego, but must be a real offering and sacrifice involving the total person—an attitude comparable to that expressed in the dedicatory prayer, "Here we offer and present unto Thee ourselves, our souls and bodies. . . ." This is an ancient Christian ritual, a "feeling after God, if perchance we might find him," but over and over again we cannot but be struck by the clarity of vision and the sincerity of earlier people.

In our text there is an indication that up to this time the gods, the potencies of the unconscious, had been undifferentiated, but that now, with the coming of consciousness to humankind, they are to be divided into pairs of opposites. Until now the gods were good-bad, favorable-unfavorable—that is, they were merely forces, like the wind or the weather—but now the beneficent gods were to be differentiated from the destructive ones.

This was the first result of the rebellion in Eden. Adam and Eve, having eaten of the fruit of the tree, called the Tree of the Knowledge of Good and Evil, began to make moral decisions based on their own ability to discriminate between the two. They had gained the power of choice. And so here, too, the task of mankind, the sole purpose of human creation, according to this account, was to make such discriminations among the gods and to bring them offerings suitable to their individual natures. So we, too, have to discover what service or gift, what sacrifice, is needed to satisfy the unconscious divine or demonic potencies within us. But to make creatures capable of consciousness, blood was needed, and the gods, being at that time the only living creations, were the only ones who could supply it. Some of them had to be killed, but none of them were willing to volunteer. So apparently Ea, god of wisdom, father of Marduk, was consulted, for we are told:

> Ea answered and spake a word unto him [i.e., Marduk],
> For the consolation of the gods he repeated unto him a word of counsel (saying):
> "Let him who created the strife be given (as sacrifice),
> I will cause him to bear his guilt, but ye shall dwell at ease."

At this the gods apparently suddenly saw a way out of their danger, crying:

> "(It was) Kingu who created the strife,
> Who made Tiamat to revolt, to join battle (with thee)."

Now this was obviously untrue. Kingu had only been created by Tiamat during the time when she was making her preparations to meet Marduk in battle. The cause of Tiamat's rebellion antedated Kingu's birth by a very long time. So he was clearly a scapegoat.

This whole episode is reminiscent of another trial and sacrifice which occurred some two thousand years later, when once more the innocent son of the mother was wrongfully accused by the representatives of the masculine deity, and his blood, too, was shed that humanity might be reborn, made new.

Then Ea fashioned mankind out of Kingu's blood and we are told Man was made for the service of the gods, and the gods were set free. This point is emphasized, for the text goes on:

> After Ea had fashioned man he laid service of the gods upon him.
> That work was past human thought, done by the cunning of Marduk
>   and the wisdom of Ea.

In this ancient account, we perceive a profound truth—that human beings were created with the sole purpose of serving the gods from whose life blood they had been formed. In psychological terms, this would mean that the physical, fleshly body is formed out of the lifeblood of the psyche, and that the sole purpose of this creation is so ego-consciousness might serve the Self. To the Babylonians it was self-evident that the spirit or psyche is anything but an epiphenomenon of the physical person. On the contrary, each of us is a psyche that dwells in a body.

Marduk then called upon the gods to build their own shrines on the earth. They were to correspond exactly to the "ways" of the gods in the heavens. These shrines are described at length in terms of astrology. The temples, called ziggurats, were built in tiers, representing the orbits or spheres of the planets. Originally, prior to 2,000 B.C., when only five planets were recognized, the ziggurats had five tiers, but later there were seven levels corresponding to the seven planets and the seven nights of the moon quarter. In the center of the court was the Apsu, container of the water of life, named for the first god, the "Abyss of Sweet Water," out of whose substance it was formed. In the great assembly hall were the shrines of the gods, each in his own constellation. Here, year by year, the festivals were held when the sun rose at the spring equinox, and the story of the creation and of the struggle between the hero-god and the primal powers, the dragons of chaos, was reenacted.

An account of the rituals that were performed on the eleven days of the New Year has been preserved in part on another series of tablets, and some of the hymns used in the liturgy have also come down to us. On the second day the following hymn was recited before the shrine of Marduk, who is addressed simply as Bel, which means Lord:

> Bel, who restored peace unto the great gods,
> Bel, who cast down the mighty ones by his glance,

> The vast heavens are the totality of thy mind.
> Bel, with thine eyes thou beholdest all things.
> Thou controllest laws by thy laws.
> Thou givest decrees by thy glance.

The statement that the heavens are the totality of God's mind is an amazingly psychological statement, and the observation that human law is subject to divine law is a truth that the present world would do well to note.

The hymn goes on to describe how Marduk cast into the fire the dragons and serpents that Tiamat's half-sister had created. There was also a tradition that he dealt similarly with Kingu. And on the next day craftsmen made statues of the Scorpion Man and the Serpent Man, two of the monsters created by Tiamat's half-sister. On the following day they were beheaded and cast into the fire.

On the fifth day, the king came to the temple. He washed his hands and knelt before the god. The high priest took the king's scepter and other insignia of kingship and placed them before Marduk in his chapel, for they belonged to the god alone and once each year the king must yield them back to him. In that moment the king was a commoner, and the high priest, representative of the most high god, smote him on the cheeks. Then, leading him before Marduk, the priest pulled his ears and made him kneel and give an account of his office.

As was customary, the confession was entirely negative. It was not a moral accounting but a recital of the prohibitions which he had or had not regarded. Just as the Ten Commandments are couched largely in terms of prohibited acts, so too the older Babylonian obligation to the gods is conceived of as the necessity to refrain from certain acts. Virtue, for them, did not as yet require a positive morality and conscious responsibility for one's motives and actions. But if such a ritual were required of all authorities today, even this degree of conscious responsibility for the office might save the world much suffering.

And so in ancient Babylon the king was required to confess:

> Not have I sinned, O Lord of the lands, not have I been negligent unto thy divinity. Babylon have I not ruined . . .
> Not have I smitten the cheeks of my subjects . . . nor caused their humiliation.

The high priest replied to this confession, speaking in the name of Marduk, "Fear not." The king, having thus rendered an account of his stewardship, received the royal insignia once again. But the law of the state presumed that the high priest had the sacred right to withhold the crown from any monarch who had abused his office. In this way the tyranny of an absolute monarchy was subject to divine law. In order to test whether the king was entirely honest in his confession, the high priest smote him again on the cheek. If the king wept, then it was known that Marduk was pleased with him. But if he did not weep, then

Marduk was displeased, and foes would surely come and cause his downfall.

Shortly after sunset on the fifth day, the priest made a fire of reeds and a bull was sacrificed over the fire. The priest and the king chanted a hymn to the "divine bull." This sacrifice recalls the epic of the slaying of the Bull of Heaven by Gilgamesh and Enkidu, his half-brother. The bull represents the zodiac sign of Taurus, the Platonic month preceding the epoch of our myth. The Babylonian and Assyrian empires correspond to the Platonic month of Aries, the Ram, which is represented by the child Marduk carrying the ram on his shoulders and was ushered in by the slaying of the Bull of Taurus, the preceding zodiac sign.

The Christian epoch that followed immediately after was similarly ushered in by the ritual slaying of a Lamb. Gilgamesh was the Bull which he himself slew, and Christ, the hero of the next *transitus*—that from Aries to Pisces—was the *Agnus Dei,* the Lamb that was slain. In the Greek Church, together with his opposite, the Antichrist, he is known as Pisces, the Fishes, ruler over the zodiac sign and Platonic month of the Fishes. At the present moment the earth is nearly out of the sign of the Fishes and is about to enter the sign of Aquarius, the Water Bearer. In Babylonian art this figure is represented by Apsu, who pours the divine water from the bowl of heaven (Figure 3). This water is Apsu himself, conquered and tamed by Ea and poured out over the whole earth, in order that human life may not be destroyed when the fiery breath of the desert dragons blow.

And so we learn from this ancient tale the oft-forgotten secret that although the turbulent and chaotic power of the unconscious may threaten the very existence of our slender and fragile conscious order, yet from the unconscious also comes the water of life, whose divine grace it is to revive us and renew our courage to persevere in the age-old struggle for consciousness.

On the last day of the festival a final hymn was sung:

> O Lord on thine entrance into thy house, may thy house rejoice in thee.
> Bring back to their places, the gods of heaven and earth.
> Let them cry to thee, "O Lord, peace!"

*

Our myth describes what might be called the "normal" course of the hero-struggle which has been waged throughout the centuries, and must be fought again by every child who would be free from dependence on the parents.

By this hero-fight the individual gains becomes free, but the archetypal image in its parental form is injured. Indeed, in our myth it is fragmented, and in the place of Tiamat—the One, the matriarchal uroboros—the company of the gods is established. They are no longer sufficient unto themselves, however, as Mother Tiamat had been, but are dependent on Man for services and sustenance.

This is an aspect of the hero-struggle and achievement that is usually not sufficiently emphasized. For it is not the archetype itself that is destroyed in the hero-fight, but its image, its *symbolic* manifestation. Some small part of its measureless energy has been wrested from it and becomes a possession of humankind, to be used for consciousness. And then the hero departs on his new way, oblivious to the fact that the archetype will surely reemerge in a new form, represented in our myth by the company of the gods, toward whom he has definite responsibilities and obligations, while the unknowable archetype itself recedes into the depths of the unconscious.

So we see that the hero has gained something in his successful struggle, but the archetypal image has been injured and must be reconstructed. This is a normal and necessary process. The hubris of the hero, the revolt against the powers of the unconscious, is the *felix culpa,* the fortunate crime.

Unfortunately, however, every child is not a hero, and not everyone has the courage to undertake the struggle for freedom voluntarily. In addition, the problem can be complicated by unusual disturbances in the image of the Father, or, even more disastrously, in the image of the Mother that one has experienced in early life.

Figure 3. Apsu pouring the divine water from the bowl of heaven. (From Stephen Langdon, *Semitic)*

4
The Development of Consciousness

In the myth, Marduk, the hero, was completely triumphant over the parent gods. He destroyed them utterly and made himself master of their powers. But he was only able to administer his new-won territories with the help of the lesser, unnamed gods. And as we have seen, he parceled out the regions among them. This he could do because he was himself one of the named gods, directly descended from Apsu and Tiamat. The named gods seem to have contained a spark of consciousness, while the unnamed gods would represent completely unconscious energies—instincts, emotions and other compulsive factors, just as the "angels" of the Old Testament and of Christianity are, as Jung points out, soulless beings, representing only the thoughts and desires of the creator.[47]

It was natural that Marduk should have authority over the unnamed gods. He had been specially equipped for his task by all the other gods, named and unnamed, who had contributed to his success. But after the fight had been won, the lesser gods, having received additional powers that they themselves had not won in battle, fell to quarreling among themselves. So Marduk had to undertake the additional task of making Man, to serve the gods and keep them content. These rival and rebellious gods represent the instinctive energies of the unconscious, and if they were to be induced to work together harmoniously, Man had to be created; that is to say, human beings had to evolve at least a small measure of consciousness. But for this, one of the gods had to be sacrificed, and Kingu, Son of the Mother, was chosen. He was duly sacrificed and Man was made out of his blood. And so Man contained the blood, or spirit, of a god.

We must pause to consider what it would mean in psychological terms that the gods war against each other, and why Marduk's first effort to bring about harmony was to place them far apart.

The gods are, of course, psychic elements, instinctive energies. In the child and in the adult, until one has developed some self-consciousness, these energies are not yet part of the conscious personality. They express themselves in compulsive emotionality—aggression, anger, love, desire, appetites of all sorts, sloth, cupidity and so on. In the human situation, the child begins life within the parental kingdom, with instinct under the control of parents and teachers. This is a situation in which one does not feel responsible for one's emotions. When the

---

[47] *Memories, Dreams, Reflections*, p. 327.

child has started to separate from parent-rule and attempts to lead an independent life, sooner or later there will arise obstacles or disasters of various kinds. Then the "gods" come into action. The individual becomes angry at events or circumstances, and when things do not change on demand one feels abused and wallows in self-pity, or blames others, turning on them with violent reproaches or aggressive action. A chaos of primitive emotions seizes the person; that is, one is back under the sway of Tiamat, and all the work must be done again.

But if, in response to an obstacle, the individual quietly sorts out his or her reactions, perhaps one might be able to set the gods far apart, as Marduk did. There is even an impulse, almost an instinct, in us to do this. Jung has called it the urge to reflection.[48] It is, perhaps, the most important civilizing element in our psychological make-up, second only to love.

For example, a man comes home from work tired and hungry to find that dinner is not ready, and his wife wants to go out while he wants to stay home. He shows his annoyance and she tries to soothe him with soft words. At this he flies into a rage, saying that she is just like his mother and he won't be managed—and goes off in a sulk. She flounces out to the kitchen and in a few minutes calls him to dinner, but he won't come, so she naturally gets annoyed too. When they finally do get together, neither will eat, but they will start to bring up all the old unresolved issues that have been repressed throughout their marriage. Yet, through all this, what the man really wants is to be understood; that is, he wants a mother. But she wants a father and will not admit it either, merely resenting her husband's inadequacy and his inability to fill the parental role.

Here again, if they could only sit down quietly and examine their reactions, separate them out so as to deal with them on their own terms, there might be a chance of resolving the difficulty and really relating to each other. But this requires sacrifice. That is, both will have to sacrifice their desire to be children, cared for by indulgent parents, and face life as it really is. If they can do this, not only will they have taken an important step toward greater self-consciousness, they will also be freed to become truly adult.

In our myth, Marduk achieved a complete victory over the parental gods, Apsu and Tiamat, but in the process of organizing the new order, Man—that is, consciousness—had to be created at a certain price, that of sacrifice, corresponding to the sacrifice of childish expectations. In the next stage of the mythologem, the story and fate of Man replaces the struggle among the gods.

The history of the gods apparently took place in an eternal time. There is no

---

[48] "Psychological Factors in Human Behavior," *The Structure and Dynamics of the Psyche,* CW 8, pars. 241ff.

mention of measured time in the story. We are told that some event or sequence of events took place "in a day when . . ."—much as in the Genesis story we are told that the creation of the universe took place in seven "days." But when Man, that is consciousness, comes on the scene, immediately there is a much keener sense of time and sequence. Time begins to be measured against the human life-span. In Paradise, before consciousness has been stolen along with the fruit of the Tree of Knowledge, humankind, like God, lived in an eternal day and did not age. But when consciousness arose, time began to move; life was no longer enclosed in a timeless "now."

The same sequence of events takes place in the child. In earliest childhood life is lived in a timeless state. Even in the early school years a summer day seems eternal. Hours and days follow each other in endless repetition. This condition persists until some event, sometimes an outer happening, sometimes an inner one, shocks the person awake; then time begins to move, events succeed each other in a recognizable continuity—memory and personal history begin, and with them there dawns a sense of responsibility for one's actions.

As the Buddhists say, for men of little intellect (or little consciousness) it is necessary to learn the law of cause and effect. This experience came to the first Biblical parents when, having eaten the fruit, they found themselves for the first time having to take responsibility for their actions. They were turned out of the Garden, expelled from the presence of God into a wilderness where they had to undertake a new way of life, dependent on their own exertions instead of being provided for by the bounty of the Garden.

The Genesis story corresponds to the history of the development of civilization as well as the development of individual consciousness. First humans gathered food, as presumably Adam and Eve did too. Then came the snaring of small animals, and later still the hunting of larger ones. In the course of long years, men learned to tame and herd certain of the animals formerly hunted, thus making the food supply much more stable. Meanwhile the women learned that they could grow the roots and berries they gathered, by scratching the ground with a digging stick. We are told that Cain, eldest son of Adam and Eve, became a tiller of the field—that is, man-like, he took over woman's invention and enlarged it by fencing in regular fields. This activity was connected with the sin of Adam, for first it was an invention—that is, a result of "knowledge"—and second, the necessity to till the ground was the form God's curse had taken.

It is interesting to note that at each of these stages in cultural development, humans felt the need to seek help from God or the gods. Even as far back as Stone Age man who painted the caves in southern France and Rhodesia, the hunting of animals was a religious task. The gods in the form of antelope or deer were propitiated with ceremonies before the hunt, just as the American Indians danced the bear dance or the deer dance before setting out to capture or kill the animal. When the hunt was successfully over, the best pieces of the meat were burnt in order that the smoke might feed their spirit-father, and the skin of the animal was used to make the ritual garments of the priest.

In the Garden of Eden, a paradisiacal condition corresponding to earliest childhood prevailed. Adam and Eve lived in the first stage, where food is available without work. We are told that God said, "Behold, I have given you every herb bearing seed . . . and every tree, in the which is the fruit of a tree yielding seed; to you it shall be for meat." (Gen. 1:29) But when they were expelled from the Garden, they were alienated from God and had to take responsibility for their own sustenance. Adam was told he would have to toil to gather food, while the punishment awarded to Eve was that she should bear children in pain. This she promptly began to do, calling her first-born son Cain. Cain grew up and became a tiller of the ground in accordance with the curse that God had laid upon Adam. So in a sense Cain took upon himself the curse of his father, the first recorded instance of the sins of the parents being visited upon the children.

The second son, Abel, was a herder of animals. Apparently this was acceptable to God, as was the killing of animals for food and as sacrifices to Himself. But the fruit of the field, the fruit of the fulfilled curse, was not acceptable to God. Cain, already rejected as the sharer of his father's curse, became violent because his sacrifice was twice rejected. This is a regular consequence resulting from a sense of alienation from God. The ego, which only emerges by slow degrees from its original identification with the Self, corresponds in the Biblical narrative to the experience of our first parents. At first they were enclosed in the Garden of Eden, entirely alone with the creator God. They were His children, made in His image, and they identified with him as children always identify with their parents.

The Genesis story is a myth of the development of the ego as a center of consciousness separate from the parents, a center that one recognizes as oneself. By an act of disobedience, independence is gained, and this is a definite step toward ego-consciousness. This is felt as a positive gain, which indeed it is. But every positive gain has a negative shadow or counterpart, and this is sensed as alienation from the parental wholeness. Adam and Eve, and Cain after them, felt themselves to be alienated from God, objects of his displeasure and his curse. In psychological terms, when the ego separates from the wholeness of the unconscious, represented by the parental home, it too feels alienated. As the old spiritual has it, "Sometimes I feel like a motherless chile, a long way from home."

In such a lament the individual, cut off from the source and origin of being, longs like a child for return to the shelter and approval of the mother's breast. Some, of course, are more robust. They experience their freedom as desirable and pride themselves on it. Still, they are not free from the negative underside of the experience that is its inevitable counterpart. In them the alienation does not merely produce a sense of loneliness and hopeless despondency. Rather, they react with anger and resentment against the parents, and with aggression and hostility against their peers. This anger is especially likely to be vented on those who have never left the parental home, or, having left it, long childishly for a return to its warmth and safety.

We are not told anything about the state of mind of Adam and Eve after their expulsion from the Garden, but Cain, their eldest son, was evidently possessed by an urgent, compulsive need to be accepted by God. He made a propitiatory gift and when this was rejected its refusal aroused in him uncontrollable emotions—humiliation, frustration and rage. Children who feel rejected by the parents may suffer from very similar emotions. On the subjective level, alienation from the source of being, that is, from God, produces a sense of impotence that in some cases is followed by collapse; in others it brings in its train an unjustified and arrogant pride that inevitably leads to hostility toward everyone.

There is yet another cause of alienation. Whenever humanity makes or discovers something that formerly belonged to the gods, we feel god-like, able to overturn nature's law. When Prometheus stole fire from heaven, he invaded the domain of the gods and infringed their prerogatives. In consequence he was alienated from them and punished eternally. Adam committed a similar sin when he took the fruit of the Tree of Knowledge and acquired the power to know good and evil. Cain's hubris consisted in learning to do what God alone had done up to that time, namely to increase the yield of the earth by farming.

From the point of view of people living in untamed nature, dependent on wild fruits and roots for their sustenance, Cain's garden, where food was to be had in plenty, must have been a veritable paradise. God had driven humanity into the wilderness, and now here was a new paradise on earth. Cain must have seemed like a god; no wonder he suffered from hubris. To this day we feel there is something dangerous about making anything that is too good, or anticipating too favorable an outcome. We fear to arouse the jealous anger of "the gods"—we do not say God, but we tap on wood or cross our fingers in the age-old apotropaic gesture against misfortune.

When Abel's sacrifice was accepted and his own rejected, Cain became violently angry and killed his brother. By this act he called down God's anger upon himself. God cursed him and drove him into the wilderness, where he could not reap the fruit of his labors, which must have added considerably to his sense of injury and injustice. But God put a sign upon him so that he should not be killed, so it looks as though God felt in some way responsible for this man, who perhaps partook of his own nature in a way that Abel did not.

Cain was punished for his hubris by being banished from God. He became the enemy of God's people, shunned by them as a murderer. This story can be taken as pseudo-history, or, if we look at it as myth, we can see in the encounter between Cain and Abel an example of the mythologem of the "hostile brothers" that is to be found in many legends, both secular and religious. From the psychological point of view this is an account of the relation of a man to his inner brother, his shadow, that part of himself that he dislikes and represses. Taken in that way, the story states that the conscious ego, represented by Cain, the elder brother, "repressed" his other side, Abel, in the most violent way, because he felt himself alienated from God on account of his successful farming enterprise, an enterprise that did not follow the traditional way of life but was an innovation. For the gods are always conservative, and must be served in the traditional manner, according to the ritual established by the Fathers. Innovations are taboo in religion; they smack of heresy. And so Cain killed Abel, and for this act he became further alienated from God and man.

This fits in with the psychological theme of the development of consciousness in the modern individual. The expulsion from Paradise is the first experience of being an individual, an "I," gained by a particular act not sanctioned by the parents. And it is almost always a painful experience. The young person who has rebelled and acted on individual initiative feels isolated by a sense of guilt. One is obliged to make one's own way, first in school and later in the greater world. A man who is successful, who marries and has a family, begins to feel very much a man. He says, "Man is master in his own house," "Where there's a will there's a way," and so on. But presently, when he begins to feel his powers waning, his hubris is likely to be followed by a depression. Nothing seems to have the old sense of importance. With Solomon of old he says, "Vanity of vanities, all is vanity." He finds himself in the wilderness where, as Kierkegaard pointed out, he suffers from a sickness unto death.

This is what might be called the normal injury to the archetypal image of Paradise, the paternal and maternal kingdom, symbolized not only by the Garden of Eden but also by the world serpent, the uroboros, that eats its own tail. Kierkegaard states that this is a universal condition, whether the individual is conscious of it or not, for everyone must inevitably become separated, detached from the primal beginnings, in order to acquire an individual consciousness.

In some cases, however, this normal aspect of the parent world has been seriously distorted, and therefore the child's inner image of the parent suffers a pathological injury. For instance, where the actual father and mother, who embody the role of the primal parents—that is, of the parental archetype—have not fulfilled their part in a positive way, but have been, perhaps, neglectful or even cruel, they will have left an imprint on the child's psyche of a destructive parental image, resulting in serious psychic trauma.

To such children God is not a heavenly father, but a vengeful, demanding and punitive Yahweh. In consequence they are cast out of the inner Paradise and find themselves in the wilderness. This happens not because of any fault of their own, but because of the pathological injury to the parental image. Experiences of this sort lie at the root of many of the problems of modern men and women.

And so we see that the mythological theme of separation from the parents has several aspects, as follows:

First, there is the normal rebellion of the child, followed by the hero-fight against the parent archetype in the form of dragon or monster, represented in the Babylonian myth by Marduk's fight against Tiamat. To emerge from dependence, the child must undertake this battle. If successful, it results in a normal injury to the parental image in the child's psyche, and in an inflation of the ego. As a result of this victory, the young person feels like an adult who can now do exactly what he or she likes, as, it seemed, the parents could previously. That is, the ego becomes omnipotent in its own eyes, and on account of this the youth is separated not only from the actual parents, but also from the supreme value of the Self. This is a condition or complex often called God-almightyness.

In the second situation, the parents have not been able to fill their roles adequately, and consequently a pathological injury has occurred to the parental image in the child's psyche. In these cases, the sense of being ostracized and alienated is naturally enhanced, so that the children begin to harbor feelings of envy and hatred toward those they consider more fortunate. This is in addition to the aggrieved sense of injustice and resentment that is only natural in all adolescents. Where these reactions are intense and deep, it is to be expected that the individuals will finally fall into despair. Where the home has been a bad one and the parents have been vicious or depraved, it is readily understandable that there should be such a result, but the parental image can also be seriously injured for a child whose physical well-being has been cared for, but who has never experienced the warmth of real love and the sense of value that results from being understood. Such a child may be psychologically injured, and may feel discriminated against, just as much as the child of a bad home. So that here, too, we have to recognize a pathological injury to the parental image.

Thirdly, there is the person who has a normal home life, has been able to leave without serious conflict, and has made a personal way in the world. He or she has even achieved considerable ego-satisfaction, and yet at about the mid-point of life feels lost in a desert where life has lost its savor and nothing matters. Perhaps it may gradually become clear that this feeling comes from being cut off from the source of life, which flows from God—that is, it arises from the unconscious depths of the psyche.

Gerhard Adler discusses such a case in his book, *The Living Symbol.* He tells the story of a woman of considerable gifts who in the midst of a successful career developed a crippling neurosis and experienced what she called "the void." She undertook an exploration of the unconscious under the guidance of Adler, and he recounts the subjective experiences she underwent during the course of her analysis, experiences that resulted in what can only be described as a rebirth of her whole personality. The experiences this woman had, and the symbols that appeared in her dreams and fantasies, correspond in an extraordinary way with the material discussed here in the final chapter.

When we see the similarity of the subjective experiences of people with very different lives, we cannot but recognize that a psychic pattern, an archetype, underlies an experience such as that of the wilderness. It is expressed not only in the story of Adam and Eve, but in many other well-known mythologems.

To sum up, a normal injury to the parental image occurs in everyone. We all have an inborn, ideal picture of mother and father, as well as an archetypal picture of the child as the center of the parents' attention—the cherished, uninhibited one, full of promise and nascent possibilities.[49] But the unconscious also contains opposite pictures of parent and child. "Parent" can mean tyranny, unlimited power and so forth, while "child" can mean helplessness and restriction. These negative aspects of the archetype come into undue prominence in the inner experience of certain people, a condition that I speak of as an injury to the archetypal image of both parent and child.

In the course of development the individual must inevitably break the tie to the parents and the childhood state. The polymorphous state of the child must give way to the one-sidedness of the adult. This is often felt as a restriction against which many people rebel. They resent their "fate." Why should they have to curb their natural desires instead of doing what they want?

But for effectiveness there must be restriction, just as in our myth the gods, in creating order, delimited their ways. If there is no restriction, then there are infinite possibilities. But the human being is not infinite, only God is, and if we are to have any relation to the infinity that is God, we must know and accept our

---

[49] [See "The Psychology of the Child Archetype," *The Archetypes and the Collective Unconscious,* CW 9i, pars. 259ff.—Ed.]

limits. Jung pointed this out in his autobiography, where he says:

> The feeling for the infinite . . . can be attained only if we are bounded to the utmost. . . . In such awareness we experience ourselves concurrently as limited and eternal, as both the one and the other. In knowing ourselves to be unique in our personal combination—that is, ultimately limited—we possess also the capacity for becoming conscious of the infinite. But only then![50]

And so a time may come to the outwardly successful person when the limitations that were once accepted become too restrictive. Life becomes sterile and one either grows increasingly rigid or has some sort of breakdown.

Sometimes this happens as the result of destructive experiences in childhood where, for instance, the tie to home and to parental love has never been adequate. In this case, pathological injuries occur to the archetypal situation. These should be distinguished from those more usual situations where the person has to break away from the containment and security of the "good" home. It takes a heroic act to rebel against kindness, and the person who has to do so will always carry a burden of guilt. The child of a dysfunctional home is spared this part of the ordeal, but instead is burdened by regret or resentment. In some cases the child is even the victim of a parent's unnatural demands or desires. Whichever form the childhood experience has taken, one is cut off from one's true self and from the most important values of life. In effect, one is cut off from God.

The realization of one's state of alienation from self and from God may not dawn until midlife, when the major tasks of outer life have been fulfilled. Then the dissatisfaction or depression is not likely to be resolved by taking up a hobby or seeking new experiences, for instance in love or travel. These are merely expedients that successful people frequently try in order to combat the depressive condition so common in midlife. In fact, the problem can only be solved by a search for the deeper meaning of life—that is, by an increase in consciousness. This has to be undertaken as a task, one that will involve an inner journey which often proves to be a veritable "dark night of the soul." In the process the ego will have to be sacrificed so that a new relation can be established with the inner "not-I," an accomplishment invariably accompanied by an experience of grace.

---

[50] *Memories, Dreams, Reflections*, p. 325.

5
Pathological Injury to the Parental Image

The Babylonian myth of the creation represents the archetypal story of the way in which consciousness gradually arose in ancient civilizations. It clearly demonstrates the great struggle that emerging consciousness had to undertake in order to free itself from the pullback into the chaotic abyss of unconsciousness, called in our myth by the names of the primal gods—Apsu, the Abyss of Sweet Water, and Tiamat, the Abyss of Salt Water.

As a result of this struggle, we are told, humanity was created and developed a separate ego capable of a certain amount of free choice. But while this development gave us some freedom, it also meant that we had to accept responsibility for our own life and fate. This naturally involved us in the problems of outer decisions and hard work, but—and this proved to be a much more serious difficulty—it laid upon us the problem of moral choice as well. In the corresponding development that must take place in everyone today if we are truly to be individuals, the ability to choose involves accepting responsibility for our decisions—for the parents no longer represent the law and are no longer responsible for its enforcement.

By "law" here, I do not mean merely the legal code, though part of the responsibility assumed by a free individual includes a right relation to the law. I mean rather the "law of things as they are"—the law, for instance, that fire burns, or that a heavy object moving at fifty miles an hour can kill or maim indiscriminately like an archaic dragon. These are laws that all must respect, and they demand a moral and responsible attitude on the part of every adult.

So when the two great potencies of the first beginning had been overcome by the actions of the hero, and their powers or some of them had been transferred to the younger gods, Marduk at once set about the task of ordering these powers by making laws to govern conduct. In order to safeguard the values that transcend individual desires, he established religious rites and sacrifices, which also served to appease the gods and make them favorable to man. The potencies that antique people called "the gods" impinge on us in the form of instinctive drives arising from the unconscious that can both threaten and replenish us.

The Babylonian myth shows how each of us can and should develop into an individual. When there has been some obstruction in the normal course of development, and one gets into difficulties and goes to an analyst for help, if one is in the first half of life this story shows in mythic form what the aim of the analysis should be: namely, that the young person should win her or his freedom not only from the parents, but also from the dominance of autoerotic and childish impulses, in order to become adequately adapted in the world.

The individual who has made good his escape from the parents must be guided in his attitudes and conduct not only by personal plans and abilities, but also by the non-personal laws and mores of society. Beyond that, we should respect transcendent values, represented in our myth by the company of the gods and the service due to them, that is, by a religious attitude.

Considerable as this achievement is, it is evidently not enough for everyone, for in the middle period of life problems may arise that call for a new solution. The diverse elements in one's psyche may produce a major conflict, or unknown parts of oneself will produce a depression, so that one loses all energy or initiative—life, outer life, is no longer challenging or interesting. When this happens, nothing less than a reconciliation of the opposing elements in the psyche will heal the conflict or release the dammed-up energies. This can only come about by working toward wholeness, which cannot be won by conscious effort alone, for the conscious ego is only one side of the psychic elements that are in opposition. When one confronts difficulties with the insight that analysis can bring, a nonrational factor in the unconscious may come to the rescue and produce a new symbol of wholeness relating to the Self.

The Self is that Completeness of each person that *The Gospel of Truth* tells us was withheld by the Father and remained in his keeping when the earthly part of humanity was led astray by Error. Man was seduced by the illusions Error produced and left the Father, so losing connection with Completeness. We are told that we can only become whole again by rediscovering the Completeness that remained with the Father: "It is a great thing that he lacks, for he lacks that which would complete him."[51]

Earlier it was pointed out that in the childhood relation to the paradisiacal condition, one felt whole on account of being identified with the wholeness of the Garden. The Garden of Eden is a symbol of the containing and nourishing mother-father world, and in the unconscious—of adults as well as of children—this favored state is represented by the parental image, and in particular by that of the Mother, who thus contains and represents the value of wholeness and of the Self. The Garden also represents the Soul, the Beloved—"A garden enclosed is the Beloved," as the Song of Solomon has it (4:12)—but to the child, and quite often to the adult as well, the Beloved and the mother-image merge into

---

[51] Kendrick Grobel, trans., *The Gospel of Truth,* p. 56. This is one of the codices discovered at Nag Hamadi in Egypt in 1945, and later published as part of *The Jung Codex.*

one another. In addition to the value of the Self, this image is imbued with the numinous quality of the deity.

The child's relation to the actual mother has a profound effect on its development, for she acts as the "evoking" factor for the archetypal maternal image. Consequently the aspect of the maternal archetype that impinges on the psyche is determined by one's personal experience of the mother. Erich Neumann points this out in his essay, "The Significance of the Genetic Aspect for Analytical Psychology," where he says:

> The transpersonal and timeless structure of the archetype, ingrained in the specifically human psyche of the child and ready for development, must first be released and activated by the personal encounter with a human being.[52]

The mother archetype represents and contains the child's wholeness, and for the child the personal mother is the embodiment of the archetype. Where the personal mother is adequate to her task and the child develops normally, slowly acquiring independence and competence in the world, a gradual separation of the archetypal value from the person of the mother takes place. She is replaced by other carriers of the unconscious value—a teacher, perhaps, or some older woman. Later this value may be embodied in a nonpersonal carrier through a religious experience. Mother Church, Holy Virgin or Christ in his role of Good Shepherd may fulfill this function for some, and in the personal experience of others, vision or dream may present these or other images as symbols of a value that cannot be grasped by consciousness in any other form.

Unfortunately, this pattern of gradual inner development is by no means always followed, and the depreciation of religious symbols that has occurred for so many people in modern times has left them stranded in a world dominated by ego values, with no guidance along the road to further development. This condition is especially prevalent among those whose childhood has been difficult and disturbed, but it is also common among those whose relation to their parents has been normal and satisfying, people who have been able to make a good adaptation in the outer world but have yet remained bound to the values of the family. These people seem to be free, but when there arises a problem of conflicting duties, one involving the claims of the family and the other the claims of the Self, they may be thrown into a devastating state. Family expectations lay down in no uncertain terms what one should do. An unquestioning sacrifice of one's personal interests in the service of filial duty is considered obligatory.

From one point of view this may be both right and reasonable. We all have

---

[52] In Garhard Adler, ed., *Current Trends in Analytical Psychology: The Proceedings of the First International Conference for Analytical Psychology,* p. 41.

obligations to our parents and family in recognition of their care and protection during our early years. This is a debt we can never discharge toward *them*, but only in our relation to a younger generation. If we look at the ethics of the situation from one point of view, we might agree that we should sacrifice our own way to take care of our parents in their time of need. But the Self may demand a different kind of sacrifice. Christ's words, "He that loveth father or mother more than me is not worthy of me" (Matt. 10:37) cannot be overlooked. But the decision to follow one's own way involves a higher kind of morality than obedience to the law. For it remains with ourselves to find out whether our impulse to go our own way, to live our separate life, is a selfish disregard of the claims of others, or whether it is truly a sacrifice of the ego and its tie to the family in the service of the Self.

Whichever way we decide, the outcome will probably make clear whether the choice was ethically right or not. And as Jung notes, we cannot escape the consequences of our choice:

> Moral judgment is always present and carries with it characteristic psychological consequences. I have pointed out many times that as in the past, so in the future the wrong we have done, thought, or intended will wreak its vengeance on our souls.[53]

But when the personal father and mother no longer embody the value and authority of the archetypal image, the individual is obliged to make a personal decision as to the right course of action for him or her; and so take a step toward the discovery of unique wholeness.

This is the second step in the hero's task. If one successfully escapes from the embracing and confining power of the parents, and especially from the mother, one will be free, it is true, but unless one undertakes the responsibility of using the power constructively to build an adaptation in the world, this will be but a Pyrrhic victory. An adequate adaptation to the outer world still leaves another and more serious problem. For in separating from the parents, and particularly from the parental archetype, one has become a free entity, but has lost the connection with wholeness. The ego is, as it were, an excerpt. The person is free, but there is a danger that this freedom may be only another way of being lost.

In the past, the symbols of religion served to relate the individual to the supreme values formerly embodied by the parents. But for many these days, religion is only an outer formality, or there is no religious teaching at all, so there are no suitable symbols through which we can relate to the wholeness from which all things come. Sooner or later, we all search for a new symbol to con-

---

[53] *Memories, Dreams, Reflections*, p. 329.

tain the unconscious values of the parental archetype if they are not to be permanently lost, leaving us adrift in an alien world. It is as if the archetypal image has been injured in the individual's psyche, not by the hero's struggle to be free, but through experiences that have either damaged the inner image or have prevented its satisfactory functioning. As Neumann points out, the maternal image activated in the child can be damaged

> through loss or disturbance of the "evoking" factor, the personal mother, which lies in her personality, or in disturbances in the world she represents. Disturbances like hunger or illness are likewise disturbances of the normal development guaranteed by the person of the mother, and the failure of the mother, for external reasons, to feed, protect and compensate, leads to a defect in the personal evocation of the mother archetype, with all the disastrous consequences this entails.[54]

Where some such conditioning has occurred, the individual will remain inwardly bound to the parental image, but in a negative instead of a positive sense. Indeed, the bond may be even more powerful, as hate can be stronger than love. The same person may harbor an unconscious image of "mother" in its most ideal form, entirely unchecked by reality. A person who has been conditioned in this way is likely to be caught in a fruitless rebellion, while at the same time longing for parental love and clinging to an inner image of an ideal parent that no one could possibly live up to. Outwardly one fights the real parents and the parental image everywhere, projected onto a human being or perhaps onto an institution, becoming one of those that Neumann has characterized as "the strugglers"— people who are ever in rebellion, but who never achieve a definitive victory, either over the parents or over their own childishness.

This is a pathological situation, and I have called the resulting injury to the inner psychic image of the parent—that is, the archetypal parental image— "pathological" too. It may occur in individual cases as a result of traumatic childhood experiences, but we find it also in whole generations as a result of the breakdown of religion and the disintegration of social mores that occurred in so widespread a fashion in the twentieth century.

In these cases the process of healing or reconstruction has to start further back, as it were, than in those persons who have had a good psychological start in life. The false or injured image has first to be dissolved, so that the archetypal image of wholeness—that is, of God as Parent—can be restored in its healthful aspect. The dissolution of the negative image corresponds to the fragmentation or *solutio* of the King that the alchemists tell of, and its reconstruction corresponds to his resurrection in purified form. This naturally comes about by means

---

[54] In Adler, ed., *Current Trends,* p. 41.

of the projection of the positive parental image onto a human being, for instance onto an analyst, with whom a relation of trust can be established. As Jung points out, "What has been spoiled by the father can only be made good by a father, just as what has been spoiled by the mother can only be repaired by a mother."[55]

Only through the experience of a positive relation to a parent, at least in token form, with all the emotions belonging to this "homecoming," can one begin to accept the life-giving power of the archetypal image. In this way one may be released from the negative and resentful spirit, this demon that possesses one and prevents the healthy use of energies. Only then can one cease wasting time on fruitless outer conflicts when what is actually involved is an inner, spiritual or psychological enemy. This in itself is a tremendous task, and it may take months of analytic work before it is accomplished, but when it is, the individual experiences a sense of well-being and renewed life, a feeling of grace and creativity, of being at last in *tao*.

Sooner or later, however, like the more favorably situated person, the renewed individual will have to break free of the longing to rest in the happiness and security of the new-found parental relation. For unless this step is taken, the individual will never find the supreme value of an individual experience of the God-image arising from within his or her own psyche. One will remain a child, whose supreme value is vested in another human being or in a symbol of the parent that embodies the image of wholeness.

And so, although it means interrupting the continuity of the theme, I think it would be best to consider this second problem first. Then when we have seen how such a psychological injury may be repaired, we can continue with our main theme, namely the problem of the nature of the new form in which the supreme archetype manifests when the parental uroboros has been split apart and the individual has gained independence from it. It really takes a potential hero to follow such a course of action, for the majority of people are content to remain childish, dependent on society or some organization to sustain them.

Even when the experience of the personal parents has been negative, there yet lies deep in the unconscious the image of the archetypal parent in its nurturing and protective aspect, together with the corresponding longing in the child to be loved and cared for. When in later life the actual parents turn to the son or daughter asking for and expecting succor, it may seem that now at last the parents will become loving because of their need. The now grown-up child feels called to sacrifice personal interests and go to their assistance, not only because duty demands it but also because of the possibility of securing their love.

---

[55] *Mysterium Coniunctionis*, CW 14, par. 232.

That is one side of the picture, and the miracle may come to pass. But it does not always work out that way. For when the archetypal image of father and mother has been split in two in the child's psyche on account of childhood experience, a return to the family in the role of benefactor or caregiver is likely to result in renewed bondage and consequent bitterness. In such cases there is no adequate mediator to stand between the human being's feeble ego-consciousness and the terrible, awesome and fascinating experience of the *numinosum*.[56] Apsu and Tiamat, chaotic abysses of water, will produce emotional turmoil if a family pattern that has been destructive in the past is reversed without a previous inner change having taken place in the persons concerned.

It is not only those who have endured traumatic childhood experiences who suffer from an injury to the archetypal image. There are many others who also find themselves astray in a lonely or terrifying world. Those who have had no real spiritual teaching or experience in youth have nothing to hold on to; life has lost its meaning. Throughout the ages the means by which humanity has made a connection between the personal ego and the forces of life that dominate the inner and outer worlds have been provided by religion and religious practices. This is taught in the Babylonian myth, where we are told that humanity was created for the sole purpose of serving the gods. The creation myths, however, are not just stories; they are concerned with the evolution of consciousness. They constitute a history of consciousness, as Neumann points out in his *History and Origins of Consciousness,* which deals with the development of human culture.

This aspect of the problem can indeed be studied as history. But this particular branch of history is not merely the story of past happenings that, however important they may have been, have been lived through and are done with, as we might assume, their achievements having become the permanent possession of humanity. In a sense this is so, but only in a limited sense, for cultures decline, barbarism reasserts itself and the achievements of the ancestors have to be won anew by their descendants. And this is inevitable, for the achievements of the race are won by individuals, and unless each gain is made good by the new generation—or, it may more truly be said, by the individuals of each generation— the ground that has been redeemed from chaos will fall again into chaos, just as cultivated land cleared by our ancestors will be again become wilderness unless it is constantly cared for.

This same law holds in the battle against unconsciousness. What has been

---

[56] [In Rudolf Otto's *The Idea of the Holy,* the word *numinosum* is used to describe the awesome emotional intensity common to all religious experience, irrespective of culture or sect.—Ed.]

achieved by our remote ancestors, whose exploits started the human race on its long journey toward culture, must be won again by each generation and by each individual who follows the hero's path. It is true that a society can be ruled by the canons of culture set up by the heroic ancestors and preserve for a while, at least in some measure, what they won by individual effort. But a society consists of individuals, and unless a sufficient number of them re-experience for themselves the struggle against unconsciousness and emerge with their own—their very own—individual value, the truths discovered by the ancestors will degenerate into convention and more or less meaningless dogma. When even these outworn rituals are neglected or forgotten, and the parents have nothing with which to replace them, the children grow up lacking an essential connection with the powerful archetypes that control life. In the case of those who were not even loved and accepted by the parents, this lack is even more disastrous.

In all such cases the child's relation to the archetypal parents, as well as to the actual mother and father, is seriously disturbed, or, to put it the other way round, the child experiences the parental archetypes in the guise of negative parents. The result may be a serious maiming of the individuality of the child, giving rise to neurosis or more serious psychological illness. Or the individual, if made of sterner stuff, may fight his or her way to freedom by sheer determination. The son or daughter may win some freedom and the ability to function more or less satisfactorily in the outer world, but eventually they will meet with many problems.

The transition to adult life is particularly difficult for such children, and usually involves crippling repressions. Ordinarily, this transition takes place without serious mishap—or we assume it does, and perhaps it did in the days when there was little disturbance in the established order and God was still "in his heaven." But today, for many people, God is no longer in his heaven, and not even in his Church. The generation brought up without spiritual teachings can hardly be expected to solve the unresolved problems their parents bequeathed to them.

In such cases a psychological analysis has to dig behind the problem of childish dependence on the actual parents. Indeed, it is probable that the individual is not consciously dependent on the parents, but may be aggressively self-sufficient. Nevertheless, beneath the negative feelings toward the parents the individual probably harbors childish expectations of the ideal parent. So the first task is to uncover these illusions in which the person is swaddled like an infant. The disturbed young people of the present generation are all too aware of their plight, and are often in despair over it. But until the unconscious illusions have been brought to consciousness, the reconstruction of the injured archetypal image cannot begin.

A college student had been doing well in his first year and the early part of the second, getting good marks and making friends, but began to slip in his work. He was unable to concentrate and realized he was in danger of failing. On questioning him I found that all his incentive had left him. He couldn't work, couldn't remember what he had learned, and quite often could not even force himself to attend classes. Meantime he had neglected his friends and other interests. When I asked what he did with his time he couldn't tell me. He just sat, or lay in bed till late in the day, and then sat up all night doing nothing. On further investigation he admitted that he had suddenly become aware of the world situation and realized, for the first time, the threat of the atomic bomb. If the world was to be blown to bits at any minute, he could not see the point of living. His anxiety was reflected in his loss of energy. His dreams were chaotic in the extreme, with visions of terror, of meaningless striving, of struggle without goal, usually breaking off unresolved. Or he would awake in fear without being able to recall the dream that woke him.

Actually, what had happened was that the archetype of order, embodied for former generations in the certainty that the world was ruled by a Heavenly Father, was no longer operative for him. Upon leaving the parental home he found himself facing the void, and the experience completely undermined him.

Today the helpful archetypal image has been fragmented for a whole generation. This is a pathological injury, not the normal one inflicted by the hero in the bid for freedom. The question we are faced with is: what happens to the archetype when its prevailing image has been overthrown.

What the outcome will be on the world stage I naturally cannot venture to predict. But I have seen a good many cases where this problem has had to be faced, and in not a few of these the effects of world unrest have been aggravated by unhappy home situations. For in the most difficult cases the parents, too, have lost their religious beliefs and are themselves disturbed. They have nothing of inner stability to give the children, and only too frequently their own disturbance expresses itself in irritability or in an indifference that stems from their deep resistance to facing their own problems.

In such cases the archetypal image of the spiritual and law-giving Father-creator and of the life-giving and sustaining Mother seems never to have been adequately formed in the child's psyche; or perhaps the innate image has suffered such mortal injury, due to the lack of parental care, that it cannot serve as a mediator between the individual and the chaotic abyss of the "time before the beginning," to use the suggestive phrase of our myth. The individual may then feel like an orphan, excluded from the family circle as our first parents were from Eden. This sense of rejection may spread out into every aspect of life, leaving the person unable to make adequate connection with anyone on a feeling basis. Adrift in a hostile world, the individual sees no reconciling symbol which might restore a sense of fellowship with others.

What can be done? Someone comes for help feeling like an outsider in every group. Such people are very difficult to deal with. Sometimes it seems that there is some truth in their assertions that others are unkind to them, and, indeed, these are not usually very pleasant people. They are suspicious, demanding, and frequently fawning in their manner; or they may be hard, aggressive and easily affronted. In either case, kindness on the part of the counselor, well-meaning attempts to show them where their attitude prevents them from making friends and so on, rarely help. The damage is too deep-seated. For when the archetypal image of the parents has sustained a serious injury, the pattern by which the individual relates to others has been evoked in a negative form. How then can this injury be healed? Is it possible for the archetypal image to be reconstructed?

This is a problem that is very common in individual cases, and as I have pointed out it lies at the root of many of our social disturbances as well. For while the failure of the human parents is the immediate cause of the child's maldevelopment, the fundamental difficulty results from a lack of connection with the archetypal parents, which goes much deeper. The prevalence of this problem is directly connected with the lack of religious experience. For the symbols of religion have, in many instances, become so depreciated that they no longer serve to relate the individual to the energy-bearing powers of the collective unconscious. Consequently one is bereft of their life-giving sustenance, while still at the mercy of its destructive power.

A long road will have to be traveled to deal with this problem. It is not usually practicable to tell the story of this inner journey. But one woman under my care drew a series of pictures to illustrate her dreams and unconscious fantasies, and these portray in objective form the way by which the psychic damage suffered to her inner image of the archetypal parent was healed.

The next chapter is about this woman's healing journey.

6
Healing the Injured Parental Image

Nora was a woman in middle life. She was married and had made a place for herself in professional work. But she had certain serious problems centering around the conviction that in every situation she was in some way "outside the circle," as she put it.

uring the course of her analysis she told me of the incident that had started her sense of being "outside the circle." As a child of about four she had gone to a party. At one point she found herself alone with a little boy of her own age, and childlike they indulged in some mutual sex play, possibly no more than some investigation to satisfy their curiosity as to how the other sex was made. On returning to the living room they found a round game in progress. The little girl was about to break into the ring when one of the adults stopped her, intending no doubt that she should wait till the game was over. But she took it as meaning that what she had been doing was so grave a sin that she could not join the other children.

Now this is a very peculiar thing about childish sexual experiences. In this case there had not been anything beyond undressing together, no actual physical contact. No one had ever told her, so far as she could remember, that such play was naughty or "bad"—a word she could never hear without having an excessive reaction. But all the same the chance action of the adult was just sufficient to arouse in her the dormant awareness of sexual instinct and its prohibition.

Such an episode could be damaging to any sensitive child. In her case it was exceedingly traumatic, because it gave form to the child's sense of rejection that actually had earlier and deeper roots, for the home from which she came was neither happy nor emotionally secure. The father was a happy-go-lucky fellow who spent all his free time and most of his money drinking with his friends at a bar, while the mother was left at home to do the work and care for the children. He was self-indulgent and lazy, caring only for his own comfort. At times he would fondle and play with his little daughter, but immediately after he would coldly dismiss her. She never knew where she was with him, but she loved him best because he was lighthearted and, at least sometimes, warm.

The mother's character was the exact opposite. She, poor woman, was strict and cold and puritanical, not sparing of criticism of her uncongenial spouse, even in front of the children. Indeed, she made Nora, her only daughter, her confidante, complaining that her father spent all his money on other women and so

99

on. Nora loved her father because he was gay and glamorous, while she respected and depended on her mother, who however was aloof and stern toward her, obviously favoring her son, whom she always indulged. There were numerous noisy quarrels between the parents which naturally increased her sense of insecurity. At such times both parents would try to bring her into their disputes, so that she felt herself pulled in two directions.

This situation is represented in her first drawing (Figure 4), in which we see the parents represented as two mountains, or two parts of the same mountain that has been cleft apart by, in her words, some "prehistoric cataclysm," while a river flows through the gorge below.

Figure 4

Nora said, "The figure stretched between the mountains is myself. The cliff on the right represents my father—but not my real father." The one on the left represented the mother. The father's rock was in radiant springtime, with trees and flowers and animals. The mother's rock was in impenetrable darkness. It was fathomless and unshaped. "But," she said, "I had been begotten from both parents and they both needed me. I was pulled and nearly torn apart."

Does this picture tell us more than Nora can say about it? In other words, is it just an attempt to draw her situation as she saw it in consciousness, or does it merit the term "unconscious drawing"? That is, does it picture more than she knows herself?

The first thing we notice is that although obviously the patient is much concerned about her difficulty, the drawing she produced was little more than a scribble. It shows neither care nor intensity. This might suggest that her concern is much more with her personal discomfort than with finding the cause of her trouble. There is no evidence of a really serious or religious attitude, a condition that will become clearer as the story goes on.

The actual father and mother were persons, not two mountain ramparts. This is a picture of the archetypal parental image, but because of the division in the family situation, the complementary wholeness that the parents should represent—making the home a secure container for the immature child—has been shattered by a "prehistoric cataclysm," as Nora said, meaning that the division took place before her personal history started, that is before she became conscious. The parents did not represent two parts of a whole to her; rather they are unrelated opposites, at odds with each other.

It is obvious that Nora as a little child could not bridge this gap in the mountain range, nor could she heal the breach between her parents. For actually she was attempting not only to bring her parents together, but also to heal an injury suffered by the archetypal image of wholeness deep within her unconscious psyche. This injury had come about, or had been constellated, because of the division in the home. And since she received no spiritual teaching as a child, there was no symbol at hand to carry the image of the Father God or the Mother Goddess that in normal cases is mediated to the child by its own parents. If she had had the image or symbol of God presented to her she might have had, even as a child, and still more likely as an adult, a means which could have served to carry her beyond the personal frustration in the home, to a relation with the source of life in the unconscious.

Nora said she was being pulled apart by the demands or needs of her parents. But the picture tells a different tale, or at least suggests a different view of the situation. Mountains don't pull. She is the only person in the picture and obviously she is doing the pulling; that is, it is her need of the parents, the ideal parents, the archetypal Great Father and Great Mother, that threatens to pull her to pieces, for her own parents could not mediate this instinctive need.

The fact that it is she herself who does the pulling is even more clearly demonstrated in a fantasy that had obsessed her from time to time, almost all her life. In it she was a child standing between two pine trees, trying with all her might to bend them together so that their tops would meet. Here again she is trying to bring together the parents, symbolized by the pine trees. This task does not seem quite so impossible as the other, but it is obviously beyond her strength. Also the symbol of the pine trees is not quite as inhuman as that of the mountain. Mountains are made of rock; they are inanimate, immovable, while the pine tree is, after all, alive. It frequently appears as a symbol of the Mother Goddess. But, as in the Attis myth, the pine tree on which Attis hangs himself represents the mother who will not allow her son to leave her. The Mountain Goddesses, however, are not involved with human beings at all, but like Annapurna, the Goddess Mother of the Himalayas, remain forever remote in their icy splendor. They are inviolate, and whoever approaches them will perish.

After this picture had been discussed, there followed several months of analysis in which Nora's present-day problems were explored, often with the help of her dreams. Her progress was intermittent. At times she would go forward, and then she would regress to her old attitude of resentment and self-pity, at which times her relation to her analyst always underwent a change for the worse. She would become suspicious, sometimes even hinting that I was hostile toward her. But gradually she came to realize that in trying to reconcile her parents to each other she had immersed herself in their adult conflicts, which did not belong to her, and so had neglected her own child's world.

She had indeed lost touch with herself. One cannot, of course, blame a child for taking such an attitude and basing her life's adaptation on it, but it has its ill effects nonetheless. And indeed this woman found herself compulsively playing the role of peacemaker in every situation of conflict she met in later life, corresponding to her childhood attempts to bring her parents together. But she remained quite oblivious to the fact that her efforts often seemed intrusive to her friends, who then naturally *did* try to keep her "outside the circle," for she had no business inside it.

When the realization dawned on Nora that she did not have to play this role any more, she experienced a great sense of relief, expecting at once to have better and more friendly relations with her companions. Then she had the following dream—or rather this is the way she told it when I asked her some months later if I might use her pictures for a lecture:

A man came and told me he could fly to the moon and back in three and a half hours, simply by using his kilt as wings. I said to him that I thought it would be better if he got a footing on the earth.

When I look up my old records, I found a certain discrepancy in her later account of the dream. I do not think Nora intentionally changed the dream. I think the change was quite unconscious and is an indication of the very thing the dream is talking about. This was the dream as she originally wrote it:

Dream of man flying to the moon. The scene took place in a house, probably mine. A man whom I liked very much and vice versa conducted an orchestra. I wanted to join it, but he said, "You are not ready." Then we both went into another room. He wore an outfit which reminded me of a Roman soldier's kilt. Pleated skirt and modern jacket. He said angrily, "I am able to fly to the moon and back and forth, but here on earth I stumbled on a dirt road."

I asked him how he managed to fly and how long it took him. He showed me the movement of his legs. This and the pleated skirt were the motor, which brought him to the moon. It took him three and a half hours. I felt the type of outfit he wore was unsuitable for the trip, and the motor he used was not workable in any way we knew. The flying time was too short. However, I did not really doubt the truth of his statement.

The reason for not doubting was that he had really been back and forth, and that it has just not even occurred to me to doubt it. Neither did it occur to me that I could have expressed my thoughts. I felt this would not have been my role.

In her later memory of the dream, Nora said what she should have said in the dream situation, a change that might be due to a wish to say the "right" thing, or it is possible that the difference really reflects an inner change of attitude that had taken place in the interval.

There are various interesting aspects of the picture she drew of the dream man in flight (Figure 5). It has much greater authenticity than the first picture. Nora was evidently "in" the experience and so made a stronger drawing.

Figure 5

The man who leads the orchestra obviously represents her animus. He is conducting the music, which refers to the feeling function, but he tells her she is not yet ready to play too; that is, her extraverted feeling is not genuine. Then he shows his character as animus, namely that he is at home in the unconscious— he can fly to the moon—but on earth he trips up and cannot manage.

At this time Nora had not entirely accepted the face that she had to take up the burden of her problem herself. She was still unconsciously blaming her parents for her difficulties and assuming that somehow life ought to make good her loss. She was still inclined to assume that intellectual understanding might bring the needed "cure." And so, in her dream, her animus tried to convince her that he could resolve the difficulty for her by an impossible feat, namely by flying without external aid right off the earth. Clearly this is a wish-fulfilling fantasy. In her later recollection of the dream she said that, when she dreamed it, she knew that this would not work. Her problem could not be resolved by flying to the moon, and indeed the animus did not offer to take her there with him, so that even if he could pull off this stunt she would be left behind. This would involve a split in herself. In the unconscious she would imagine she was free, but in reality she would still suffer from her troubles.

Proverbially, to go to the moon or to cry for the moon means to long for the impossible. In Nora's dream the animus said he was actually able to do this. The moon represents the Eros principle. It is the abode of the Mother Goddess, who rules love and relationship. If the animus should succeed in reaching the moon, then in real life Nora would feel herself to be above sit all, safely on the moon, from where she could look down on all those benighted people caught up in life's difficulties on earth and feel sorry for them. The problem resulting from the lack of love in her childhood would be magically solved.

Shortly after, Nora had a dream in which she had just been married, though there was no bridegroom in the dream, and she suddenly realized that it was a bogus marriage. However, her mother, who was present, assured her that it must be legal because she had "paid the proper sum."

To be married would mean the union of the conscious ego with the unconscious, a step toward wholeness. Here, however, there is no bridegroom, no representative of the unconscious animus. Her mother—the one who was so lacking in real feeling—says that such a union can be bought by paying a fee. This again is a totally wrong attitude.

The dream continued and Nora found herself at a party, presumably the wedding reception. But she was alone. Everyone except her had found a partner and left. She was very unhappy and wanted to go to her mother, "at least to be with her." The dream changed then and suddenly she was with me, her analyst. "There was a mutual embrace. Warmth flowed back and forth between us. It seemed to me that you looked different, warm and alive." Formerly she had thought of me as cold and aloof. Now she discovers in her dream that it is not I who was cold, but herself.

Actually, the feeling she customarily expressed not only to me but also to her friends and acquaintances, was not genuine feeling for the other person. It was merely a manner, an animus ruse, a trick designed to attract warmth and affection. This was quite a cold-blooded attitude, a fact of which she was of course quite unconscious. This coldness had been projected onto (or mirrored in) her analyst. But when, in the dream, she recognized her own need and unhappiness and sought out her mother, "at least to be with her," immediately the analyst appeared and was seen as kind and warm.

In Nora the archetypal image of the Great Mother had been injured on account of her childhood experience of her personal mother; it had taken on the aspect of the coldness she had actually experienced, and this had been projected onto me. But when Nora herself changed in her attitude, the mother image turned a different face toward her. Her actual mother, of course, was not changed by the dream, nor had I changed. It was Nora's emotional relation to the archetypal image of the mother that had changed, so that she could express real feelings toward the analyst, at least in the dream.

The next night she had a dream in which she was in a hotel with her father and mother. They were about to leave the hotel. Everyone was ready except her. She could not find her suitcase to pack. She became panicky and ran around crying and shouting, completely beside herself. "The prevailing feeling," she said, "was that I had to accomplish something I was not able to do. The effort and the desperation were beyond description."

This dream brought up the memory of an incident that had happened when Nora was about twelve years old. She had gone to the mountains with her parents for a holiday, when she was suddenly taken ill with acute appendicitis. They started for home to find a doctor. It was a long way to the train station and they arrived before the express was due, so they went into the restaurant for lunch. When the train came in, her father would not leave his unfinished meal, although Nora was in great pain. Because of his delay they missed the train and had to wait several hours for another. When they finally reached home, Nora had to be rushed to the hospital for an emergency operation. And so this dream recalls the lack of love she had experienced as a child, not only from her mother but still more from her self-indulgent father.

The dream situation is somewhat different, for there she is struggling to accomplish a task that in reality is perfectly simple and ordinary, namely to pack her suitcase. But in the dream it seems to be impossible and produces an unreasonable amount of emotion and panic. A dream picturing frustration of this kind usually indicates that one's conscious purpose is opposed by a very strong unconscious pull in another direction. In the dream Nora is unable to gather her possessions together, and so she is faced with a dilemma. Either she must stay and collect them and let her parents leave without her, or she must leave her possessions and go with her parents.

I am inclined to think that in this case the possessions represent those things that really belong to herself, while the choice she has to make is whether to go with the parents—that is, to remain as a child, so losing a part of herself—or to let them go without her in order that she may find what really belongs to her as an individual.

This series of dreams was followed in reality by the first expressions of genuine affection and trust toward me, her analyst, and she even gained a hint of understanding of the inner values her relation to her analyst embodied. A week later she had a dream of self-dedication and the acceptance of death, and this was followed by a dream of the birth of a baby, in which she offered "a prayer of thanksgiving and self-surrender." The acceptance of death naturally did not mean physical death. It symbolized the death or surrender of the ego. And the birth of the baby represented the coming of a new self, perhaps even a forerunner of the capital-s Self, organizing center of the psyche.

It was at this point that Nora gave me the incorrect version of the dream in which the animus claimed to be able to fly to the moon. She said that she had told the man in the dream that she thought it would be better if he stayed on the ground, which was not the fact. This was a piece of self-deception that was sure to have unfortunate consequences. Indeed, almost immediately she fell into a regression. All her old cynical atheism came up again, together with a great distrust of both her analyst and the analytic process. Then there followed dreams in which she herself was flying.

A few days later, in a vision, Nora saw the two mountain cliffs of the earlier fantasy, and again found herself being pulled apart. She described it like this:

> But now the pull from the mother was stronger. I was pulled away to her side. [Evidently the experience of feeling and trust toward her analyst, transient as it had been, yet continued to act in the unconscious.] I went from sunshine outside, into darkness inside [Figure 6]. There, in impenetrable darkness, I saw my mother sitting. She had covered her face with her hands and was crying. I knelt down by her side and said, "Don't cry, mother. I am going to stay with you."

In the previous dream she had said she wanted to find her mother because of her own need to be with her. So things have got a bit mixed up here: it is not clear which of the two is in need of the other. The dream continues:

> Suddenly large green eyes come toward me through the darkness. It is a huge snake that coils around us until we are completely surrounded by it, like a tower on a grave.

Figure 6

This great snake is the unconscious in its maternal form, the uroboros, and both mother and daughter are enclosed in its embrace. The question of who is doing the pulling is now answered: there is a mutual instinctive attraction and identification between them. They are quite undifferentiated and form a mother-child unity. They are but two aspects of the eternal feminine. Such a situation means the complete loss of all individuality. But this woman had taken at least the first steps toward individual development through her analysis. So the fantasy continued:

> Then I was standing in front of the tower of snakes, not knowing what to do. [It looks as if she is at one and the same time both inside the uroboros and outside it. This means that at least a part of her is now outside the identification with her mother.] Suddenly Dr. H and Dr. X [a former analyst] were standing beside me, one on each side. They each put an arm around my shoulders and we approached the dragon [Figure 7, next page].

It looks as if, with the help of the two people who have understood her problem and offered her disinterested help, she may be able to confront the archetypal problem that was the cause of her neurosis.

The next fantasy showed the mountains again (Figure 8, next page). But now the mother mountain has become green, and there is a pine wood on its lower slopes, showing that the feminine side of life is no longer a mysterious and unfathomable darkness; it has become beautiful and welcoming. On the summit of the mountain stands a church, showing that Nora is beginning to realize that her problem with the mother and her longing for mother-love is fundamentally a religious one, to be resolved through a relation to a suprapersonal value.

Figure 7

Figure 8

Instead of her own child-figure stretched, as though crucified, between the mountains, she saw a figure of the Buddha, enclosed in a circular design. It was really more like a design than the picture of a person or statue. It seemed to be floating in the middle of the chasm. At first she thought that surely the Buddha, the enlightened one, would be able to heal the breach that separated the mountains, and this would be the answer to her problem. She would adopt his attitude of detachment and all would be well. But then she remembered that on a former occasion she had said to me that the Buddha's attitude of renunciation and non-identification was the highest possible achievement. To which I had replied that that might be so, but we had to begin right where we were. If we are still caught in the emotional desires and drives, we are not disidentified and it is no good trying to base a solution for our lives on such an illusory freedom. We must build on the ground. You cannot build a skyscraper beginning at the fiftieth floor, but only from a foundation deep in the earth. Adopting the Buddha's attitude would be equivalent to the earlier image of flying to the moon.

So when she looked at her picture again, she decided to discard the ghostly Buddha and the fantasy of solving her problem by identifying with him. In her imagination she then constructed a rustic bridge across the chasm. But this too was only a wish-fantasy, for when she tried to cross the chasm on this bridge, she felt as if the mountains were pressing together to crush it and her.

Then in her fantasy the mountain masses did crash together. The bridge was crushed and she herself was thrown down into the abyss (Figure 9). To her amazement she was not killed, but found herself standing on a black square below the mountains. The river now flowed through a tunnel which penetrated

Figure 9

them (Figure 10). One other thing she observed. She was now no longer a child, but an adult. The place where she was standing was black and she still felt the crushing power of the mountain movement, for although the peaks had come together, it seemed as if their momentum would overflow and crush her. So in her fantasy she ran up one of the paths, which only now she saw wound up each of the mountains. She hid behind a pine tree, clinging to its trunk for support. Then the mountains came together with a crash, producing a flash of fire, like lightning, that burned up and died down (Figure 11).

She returned to the former spot to look, almost in despair, wondering how she could get past this mountain barrier. Then it occurred to her that if she went up one of the paths she would be able to climb over the massif and continue her journey. She decided to take the "mother" path. In this way, for the first time in her life, Nora accepted the fact that she was really a woman and had a right to her own feminine instincts.

I need hardly say that this was a most important and releasing experience, but it did not solve the major problem of feeling herself to be an outsider. For this a further experience was needed and, after a time, the dreams and fantasies started up again. Once more she saw the black region at the foot of the mountains. It was night and she was on the wrong side of the river. She would have to cross it if she were to be able to climb the "mother" mountain. And there was no means by which she could get across. Then she saw a knight in shining armor come and kneel before the "father" mountain (Figure 12, page 112), as though he had realized he could not overcome it by direct attack and so was praying to it or beseeching it not to obstruct the path. But it remained like an immovable rock. Neither his sword nor his prayers had any effect on it.

Then the knight disappeared and she found herself before the rock, pushing it. (Figure 13, page 112), trying to get it out of the way by sheer physical force, but of course she was quite powerless to do so. And not only was *she* pushing the rock, but a great nebulous female figure that stood behind her was pushing her toward the rock. Apparently this is the same colossal figure made by the serpent that coiled around her and her mother in one of the earlier fantasies. She did not feel that this figure was helping her in her efforts to move the rock, rather she felt herself to be crushed between the two forces. "I was in despair," she told me, "because I was not able to move the rock and because of the pressure from behind." Indeed, she felt herself in danger of being entirely crushed.

So she was at last caught, pushed on by her own feminine nature, which she had recently accepted, here represented by the female figure that seems so huge and unrelenting because it had never been adequately embodied for her in a human person. She was caught between this figure and the rock, representing the

Figure 10

Figure 11

Figure 12

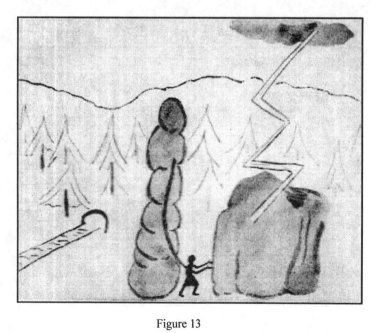

Figure 13

father, that seemed to her like the fiat of the Old Testament God. She could neither overcome the masculine power nor deal with it in a feminine way. And, too,
she could no longer jump over the difficulty, as she had repeatedly tried to do in
the past, by an animus flight, for now the fact that had already accepted her
femininity held her to the ground. At last she realized that fantasy solutions will
not work, that what she needed was a *real* solution based on reality.

The active imagination continued:

> Suddenly a stroke of lightning struck the rock and broke it into a thousand pieces
> [Figure 14, next page]. A voice said, "You are free, if you wish to be." Then a
> warm feeling flowed through me. I kneeled down and said, "Don't leave me alone.
> I love you." The tower replied, "I'll stay within you. There will be somebody else
> helping you." The foggy image melted in the ground and instead Dr. Harding
> stood there [Figure 15, next page]. She said, "Come, I'll help you across the river.
> Take a piece of the rock with you, one that has the mark of the lightning on it. It
> will guide you."

And there the fantasy ended.

This was obviously a very important experience, and we must examine it in
detail for it represents the solution of the first part of Nora's quest. The alchemists called this the "lesser work" that results in the formation of the "white
substance" or the "White Queen," representing the feminine or Eros value. For a
man the White Queen would stand for the anima in her royal aspect; for a
woman it means the coming to consciousness of her womanly nature. This corresponds to the development of what I have called the Eros-woman, to distin-
guish it from the earlier stage in the development of a woman's personality,
when she lives her femininity unconsciously and so personifies the man's ideal
of woman and adapts to life as if she were the man's anima.[57]

In Nora's fantasy she is once again on the "father" side of the river, and is
confronted by the father-mountain. This is clearly not just a symbol of her own
father, but is rather a manifestation of the Father, the masculine Jehovah God
who looms over her, blocking her path. In her actual life it made itself felt as the
cause of her difficulties in the outer world, and more especially it prevented any
sustaining belief in God as friendly or helpful. Indeed, in one of her bad moods
Nora repeatedly declared that there was no God, no divine spirit in the universe
or in the psyche either. Consequently in her fantasy God appears to her like an
immovable and threatening mountain. For it is quite useless to deny that there is
a power creating and controlling life. There manifestly is. No matter what we

---

[57] [See Harding, *The Way of All Women: A Psychological Interpretation*, esp. chapt. 1,
"All Things to All Men."—Ed.]

Figure 14

Figure 15

call it, there is without a doubt a creative force in the universe and within ourselves as well. So this fantasy was concerned with the problem of overcoming her wrong conception. She was completely blocked, she could not go on. But a knight in shining armor appeared as if to solve her problem for her.

This was the third time that a magic way out of her dilemma had been proposed by the advent of an animus figure. The first was the man who offered to fly to the moon and back; that is, he suggested that *she* might fly to the moon, realm of the Eros principle, or that *he* might, which would mean she would acquire feminine values through the animus. This obviously would not solve the problem, and she showed him that it would be better if he would only stay on the ground—a piece of advice that she was compelled to follow herself later in her fantasy. Then when she found herself still trying unsuccessfully to bridge the gap between the father and the mother worlds, she made a picture of the Buddha, whose teachings of disidentification seemed to offer a way out. But when she tried to separate herself from all emotion, she found that the isolation that had been the core of her distress all along only deepened. And now, when once again she was faced with this seemingly insoluble problem, a knight in shining armor arrived.

The knight would be the personification of the knightly spirit of the age of chivalry, a Christian hero-figure. But his sword and shield were quite useless against a mountain. In other words, the kind of religion, the attitude toward the spiritual world, of the Middle Ages is of no use in her situation. In the time of the knights, the unconscious part of the psyche was projected into the heavens and the forces of the unconscious were hypostatized. To that age, God and the angels and devils were living entities, metaphysical realities that no one questioned. But to a modern woman with a skeptical turn of mind such a solution would be as futile as a tin-foil sword against a mountain. The only hint that the appearance of the knight gave her of a right way to approach her problem was that he knelt. That is to say, he took a reverent attitude when he realized that force was of no use. She took the hint and in another picture (not reproduced here) she is shown kneeling.

After this Nora found *herself* confronting the great rock, as if she realized that she could not solve her problem by proxy, but must undertake the task personally, stripped of all animus defenses and aggressions. And she must face the ordeal in all her feminine vulnerability. But no longer was it a mountain that confronted her; it was a rock, huge it is true, but less than a mountain. So her attitude of humility and reverence for what the rock embodied—the unknown Father God—had had the effect of reducing the size and threat of the mountain.

At this point in the fantasy, the mother mountain appeared in the form of a nebulous black figure that pushed her on to attack the rock herself. But she, small and feeble as she was, was quite unable to move it, even though she was pushed on—or might not one rather say, backed up?—by the mother mountain. Formerly she had been pulled apart by the action of the two mountains. Now it seemed that she was to be crushed between them. Does this not suggest that all along her attitude had had something to do with the form in which the parental archetypes presented themselves to her? Nora's attitude had changed materially through her analytic work, and correspondingly the problem, or the archetypal image in which it was represented, had changed too.

This form of the experience of mother and father as of enormous size, immovable and adamantine, could not be dealt with or resolved by her unaided strength. Formerly she was a passive victim, now she had tried to exert her personal power and the one was as futile as the other. The father rock was indeed not moved. But something happened that *she* did not bring to pass: the rock was split into fragments by a stroke of lightning.

I think this means that when she could accept her human limitations and stop trying to resolve her difficulties by magical means or by ego-power, there came a flash of insight. The unseen and unrecognized spirit, whose very existence she had so often denied, struck. But it was not she herself who was blasted for her arrogant attitude. No, the lightning struck the rock and shattered it. Her conception of the divine spirit of life as a tyrannical father was shattered by a flash of insight into its true nature; or it might be said that the stroke of lightning represents a flash of understanding, or a blaze of emotion, that broke up her identification with the father and released her from the domination of a Jehovah-like God through a shattering and painful experience.[58]

But note that she was not left alone in her distress, nor was she left without guidance. For there remained some fragments of stone marked by the lightning. She is told to take such a piece and that it would guide her. This piece of the rock would represent the core of her experience that had the mark of deep and painful emotion, as well as the impact of the moment of insight that came to her in a flash. This stone, this memory, she was told she must cherish.

At that same moment, the mother megalith melted away and was replaced by a human figure. The stone mother became human—a feminine figure corresponding to the dreamer's own femininity. The father mountain, in contrast, had been replaced by a fiery spirit, corresponding to the spiritual nature of the true animus of woman. The feminine figure that replaced the mother mountain was

---

[58] [Jung: "Lightning signifies a sudden, unexpected, and overpowering change of psychic condition." ("A Study in the Process of Individuation," CW 9i, par. 533).—Ed.]

not her actual mother, nor was it her analyst onto whom she had projected the mother value, although it seemed to have her form. For the voice that spoke out of it promised to be *within* her, guiding and helping. It is obviously the voice of that feminine value that was embodied for her first in her own mother and later projected onto her analyst. But this value she was told was now to function within herself, as an inner guide and companion. Meanwhile, the outer great adamantine image had dissolved, leaving the figure of the analyst as an ordinary human being—truly an ordinary human being, yet one who had been able to act as guide during all this long transition.

There was another interesting point here. When Nora first went over to the mother mountain, being pulled by the stronger force, she had knelt beside the mother and said, "I will never leave you," as if she were the mother of her mother. Now the situation is reversed. It is she who prays, "Don't leave me. I love you." And the voice answers, "I'll stay within you." Not with you, but *within* you! It is this same inner voice that told her to take as her guide a piece of rock that was marked by the fiery experience. This would become a sort of touchstone that would tell her what was true and what false, and in any conflict or uncertainty she could and must consult it. For where the fire is—that is, where in the future she feels a genuine flash of emotion and a numinous presence—there she will have to go, regardless of whether it is convenient or not, and regardless of whether it is difficult or painful or unpopular, for there lies the road marked out by the spirit of the true God. Just as Jesus said in one of his apocryphal sayings: "Whoso is near to me is near to the fire."

In actual life, this would mean that whenever Nora was in doubt, this stone that has been marked by a burning and numinous spirit will guide her. She must search within herself for the indications marked by this kind of intensity. They may come as desire, or longing, or perhaps as fear or some other emotion. These will enable her to discover which impulse is from the Self and which from the ego or from some conventional obligation, or possibly from some childish or slothful desirousness.

Where a conflict of duty arises within one, one should try to find out where the numinous value lies and to follow it. For instance, the expectations of the family and the claims of one's own inner way may clash and there seems no way of telling which obligation should be accepted and which refused. Loyalty to the family, perhaps the need of an aged parent, may call one to give up one's own life, but if the fiery stone clearly shows that in order to follow the call of the Self one must leave the family, then even this sacred duty must be laid aside. For if one goes back to the family with what Erich Neumann has called "illicit compassion,"[59] one's altruism will defeat one's own sacred responsibility. Just as Psyche, when seeking the treasure from the underworld, was warned to disregard all appeals to her compassion, so we must follow her example. But it must be only on the quest for the treasure of the Self that we disregard appeals to our charity. To disregard them merely to satisfy our own selfish and autoerotic wishes would not lead to salvation, nor to the recovery of the treasure; it would lead only to spiritual death.

And so Nora was told that a true decision could only be made by the touchstone of the lightning, the numinous experience. Without it, one would do well to follow the advice of the wisest counselor one can find. For the road to individuation cannot be followed by children.

This most instructive series of dreams and fantasies shows how the archetypal parental image, that had been seriously damaged for this particular woman, was restored or reconstructed through the experience of analysis. In her relation to her analyst she had found a bridge to the inner experience of the Great Mother that would bring her the values of Eros and the renewal of her life; and, too, the terrible image of the Jehovah-like God was replaced for her by a spiritual insight that would serve her as guide on her way.

Thus the first part of the task was done. The pathological injury to the parental image had been restored, and Nora was now in a position to rebuild her relation to people and to the external world. Whether this degree of development would prove to be sufficient to satisfy the needs of this particular woman remained to be seen. She was no longer under the compulsion of her negative relation to the parents, and she no longer felt herself excluded from every warm human group, but of course this did not mean that she would live "happily every after," as in a fairy tale. The inner experience would have to be made good in actual living.

Nevertheless, an experience such as this is in a sense definitive. Nora could never be quite the same again. And some day, perhaps, the call would come to her to undertake the further task of finding an individual relation to the numinous value that had been revealed to her. It is this great work, or opus, that Jung called the process of individuation.[60]

---

[59] *Amor and Psyche,* pp. 48, 112.

[60] [Jung: "The opus consists of three parts: insight, endurance and action. Psychology is needed only in the first part, but in the second and third parts, moral strength plays the predominant role." *(C.G. Jung Letters,* vol. 1, p. 375)—Ed.]

7
The Return Home

In the preceding chapter we saw how the subjective injury that Nora had received as a result of her childhood experiences had affected the image of the Mother and Father archetypes in her psyche. That is to say, the ontogenetic, personal aspect of the archetypal images had been injured or disturbed for her. We also saw how, as a result of her analysis, this injury was gradually healed and positive images replaced the damaged ones.

However, something further was accomplished by the analysis, for the symbols that occurred in the last series of fantasies were not just of a loving human father and mother restored to her, as if she were a child again. If this had been so, she would have been left in a condition of childish dependence on her analyst, as a mother surrogate, and this was not the case. The symbol of Mother as a personification of the feminine wisdom within herself, and of the Father as a stone marked by lightning so that it had a spirit in it, were numinous. They produced in her a sense of freedom and inner autonomy she had never experienced before. And as a result of these deeply moving subjective events Nora became, for the first time in her life, truly an individual.

To recapitulate, during the course of her analysis two processes had gone on in Nora simultaneously. She had gradually come to see that the lack of an adequate relation to a positive mother figure was the cause of the difficulties in her relations with other people. She realized that the lack of rapport with others could not be overcome by conscious effort, nor could it be adequately compensated by identification with the animus. Her inner insecurity, augmented by her unconscious sense of guilt arising from the childish sexual play, had resulted in alienation from her own feminine nature, the source of feeling and relatedness. This had caused a serious deformation of her character. It had meant that, instead of basing her human relationships on genuine feeling, she had acted on animus ideas of feminine behavior.

But an *idea* of feeling is the opposite of real feeling, and so it alienated instead of uniting. This realization was not merely an intellectual one, though understanding was a necessary part of the process. The realization went much deeper than that, involving her whole being. As a result of this change, she was able to renounce the old way of functioning through animus magic. Even the "white" magic, represented by the knight in shining armor, had proved helpless before the obstacle in her path. But when she experienced a true turning of the heart, then things changed, as if by a miracle, one not wrought by animus magic.

While this change was occurring, another was taking place without which the inner transformation would have been impossible. This deeper change concerned her relation to her analyst, onto whom she had projected the archetypal image of the mother, while at the same time she recognized her as an individual too. The dreamer's relationship to her analyst had been quite ambivalent at first; sometimes it was positive, at others distrustful and even hostile. But gradually this had changed. She became able to give up her animus attitude and accept her own femininity. As a result her relation to her analyst became established, and she found she could accept her loving feelings for her without demanding that the analyst must love her first and in the particular way she wished.

The image of the archetypal parents that had dominated Nora's psyche in a negative and destructive form had been overcome. In its place, she experienced not only the positive parental images in her relation to her two analysts—one a man and the other a woman—but she also learned in the final active imagination that this value did not come from the analyst but from a guiding and protecting element that would now function from within herself. She had at last found and recognized the Great Mother within and, at the same time, had found and recognized her own femininity as a value to be prized and relied on.

Such a transformation corresponds to the culmination of the myth of Demeter and Kore, when the young woman, the Kore, represented by Persephone, the daughter, becomes Demeter, the mature maternal goddess who will herself re-live the myth with a new Kore. A similar process is shown in the pictures on the walls of the initiation chamber in the Villa dei Mysterii in Pompeii, as previously mentioned. In Nora's case, this transformation took place in her analysis.

The father-image, too, was transformed. This is a woman's psychology, so while the stone-like mother-image had become human, the father-image had changed in a different way. The rock that represented him had been shattered by a bolt of lightning, and a fragment of the rock had been marked by the fire from heaven. Nora was told to take this stone with her as a guide. The father had thus become spirit, but spirit still embedded in stone. This means that the assimilation of spirit into her own psyche was not yet fully accomplished, and the reconciliation to God as Father—that is, in his aspect as the positive masculine spirit, or Logos—was still represented for her by the marked stone, rather than coming to her as an inner voice. But the stone, as the voice of the fantasy told her, would act as a touchstone by which she could determine what was true and what was false in the spirit realm. And so Nora would no longer need to depend on the magic-producing animus for guidance.

The pathological injury which the parental image had suffered in this woman was healed. The archetypal image of the parents had been reconstructed and the hero's struggle for release from the positive parents now confronted her. The way was open for the next step in her development, namely the search for a new symbol that might represent and contain the supreme value that was no longer carried for her by the parental image.

This next step would inevitably involve a new injury to the archetypal image, corresponding to the one inflicted by the youth who frees himself in order to depart on his own adult adventure. But this is a normal injury. For obviously, where there is no longer a child then the *role* of parent is nullified. The value the parental image carried, and its energy, must go elsewhere and find a new expression. This necessity recalls Christ's statement about the new revelation he brought: "Neither do men put new wine into old bottles: else the bottles break, and the wine runneth out . . . but they put new wine into new bottles." (Matt. 9:17) The old form of the parental image is inevitably injured by the growing-up of the child, but this injury is necessary and normal, and the child's act of disobedience, corresponding to the overcoming of the parents by the hero, is the *felix culpa,* the fortunate crime.

In her quest for individuation, Nora had accomplished this much. She would now have to undertake the next stage, one that would free her from dependence on the emotional support and wisdom of her analyst. This task corresponds to the exploits of the mythical heroes who, like Marduk, fight and overcome the parental monsters who would hold them forever in bondage.

If we transpose the hero myth into the terms of our own inner myth, we see that the God-image in its primal or infantile form must be overcome by the young person who would truly become an individual. Those who are successful become heroes, who can then step out into their own reality, their own individual relation to the world. No longer will they be restricted by the rules the parents made, nor supported by them. For better or for worse, the gods of the first beginnings no longer rule their lives. Desirable as this freedom may seem, to achieve it involves a life and death struggle, not only against the parents but also against one's own infantility—a struggle in which only some are victorious, and others are defeated.

This inner battle for freedom and for one's own individuality takes place in stages. It is not achieved in one supreme effort. The child emerging into adolescence begins to criticize the parents, seeing that they are not infallible but often make mistakes. At first the child complains or berates them for their inadequacies, but later understands that they are not gods but simply human. In 1959, in a filmed interview, Jung told of the way in which this experience came to him.

One day he seemed to step out of a mist and suddenly become conscious of himself; he was separate from his parents, and for the first time he was able to evaluate them as individuals.[61]

When consciousness thus dawns, one looks around and sees that "things" did not come into existence by themselves, that they were not always and forever there. The realization dawns that someone, some human agency, must have created and ordered them.

Unfortunately, this is an achievement, an enlightenment, that is not always accomplished even by grown men and women. More than once I have heard an adult assert, "But life owes me that!" We are not surprised that the infant merely cries for food when hungry and that its cry seems to produce milk, because it knows nothing and cares nothing for the history of its arrival, all nice and warm in the breast or bottle. The infant's concern is simply and solely with the comfort or discomfort in its stomach. The ten year old returning home from school and calling out, "Mum, is dinner ready?" has little more awareness of cause and effect and of the mother's work than does the infant, though intellectually able, perhaps, to tell you how food is produced and cooked. But psychologically the child is naive. Dinner just *is,* a fact respondent to one's needs. Consciousness is so dim that it cannot penetrate beyond subjective acts or feelings.

At adolescence one begins to rebel against parental control, demanding freedom without realizing its related responsibilities. Indeed, this demand usually includes the expectation that one has a right to the family assets (such as the car). This unconscious demand often persists through college and even beyond. Usually, however, on leaving college the young person will have to start out independently and will then be confronted, as Marduk was, with the unordered multiplicity of the world. It becomes necessary to capture or exploit the riches of the environment, and to order and control them in the interests of one's personal life. In the greater world a person is judged by what she or he does. Excuses are not acceptable. This is often especially difficult in the emotional sphere, where a high price is exacted for indulging in moods.

Marduk did not celebrate his victory with an orgy, nor did he consider that he had the right to rest on his laurels. He immediately started to make laws to control himself as well as the gods. We are told that he invented many "cunning" plans to take care of all the situations that pressed upon him once the old order had been dispersed. And just so, in the personal history of each one of us, after

---

[61] [See "The Face to Face Interview," with John Freeman, BBC television, in William McGuire and R.F.C. Hull, eds., *C.G. Jung Speaking:Interviews and Encounters,* pp. 425f.; also Jung, *Memories, Dreams, Reflections,* pp. 48f.—Ed.]

we have freed ourselves from the parents sufficiently to have at least a glimpse of their reality as individuals, we must begin to find a place for ourselves in the world as separate persons, taking responsibility for our own lives—earning a living, adapting to society, marrying, bearing and rearing children, and assuming our share of the collective burden of a civilized society, which also in turn ministers to our needs.

This is the task of the first half of life, and it may be regarded as the usual way of development, though many people fail in it, partially or completely. We find many childish adults who still unconsciously live in a father-mother world. They are the *puer aeternus* type of man and the anima type of woman,[62] and they form a considerable proportion of the people who seek analysis in the first half of life, when the major problems are concerned with winning freedom from the parents and making an adequate adjustment to life.

We must not make the mistake, however, of taking these goals merely in their external aspect. To leave home and get a job, even to be successful in a worldly sense, does not necessarily mean that one has freed oneself from the parental world. It is possible to be outwardly free while remaining inwardly contained in the family. In such cases the analysis of the problems belonging to the first half of life may have to be carried out with older persons too. With young people it may be sufficient to help them gain their outer freedom, leaving the deeper task to be accomplished later, when life itself will have brought home to them the realization that everything is not in order. But with older people this is not enough. Analysis of persons in the first half of life, or of those who have carried the problems of youth unresolved through the years, will be concerned first of all with this issue. Its resolution is usually accomplished through the projection of the parental image onto the analyst, where the difficulties due to the analysand's unresolved fixation—to the parent and to one's own infantility—can be worked on and overcome.

Even in an individual whose relation to the parents has been fundamentally sound, where there has been love and mutual understanding, there is likely to come a time when the young person begins to resent what he or she feels to be unjust demands for obedience on the part of the parents. When a situation of this kind produces so much difficulty that the person goes into analysis, release will come through the realization that negative feelings and resentment really derive from one's attitude rather than from any real hostility on the part of the parents.

---

[62] [See Marie-Louise von Franz, *The Problem of the Puer Aeternus.* An "anima woman" is one who is content to fulfill a man's expectations of her; see Harding, *The Way of All Women: A Psychological Interpretation.*—Ed.].

One will then no longer have to fight *them,* but can overcome them by over-coming one's needs for support and protection. Having realized this fact, a person will then be ready to launch out into life, with every prospect of making a successful adaptation, both in the world of work, the masculine world of the Father and of Logos, and also in relationships, which belong to the feminine realm of the Mother and of Eros. In this way the task of the first half of life may be accomplished, the first stage of the hero-adventure fulfilled. It is a task that usually takes a person to the age of about forty, but then a new movement of the life energy begins to enter the picture, and we come to the second stage of the hero-adventure.

Normally, during the first half of life the personal parents, as the carriers of the archetypal image, are replaced by symbols of the Great Mother and the Spiritual Father, embodied in new and less personal form. On the extraverted side, if one is so fortunate as to have a satisfactory spiritual experience—and by this I mean a genuine inner experience—then the institutions and the symbols of religion, including divine figures felt to have an objective reality, may replace the parents in one's life, and carry the value they no longer embody.

But not infrequently, around the middle of life these symbols fail to satisfy the demands of the psyche. The libido begins to withdraw from outer activities and the realization forces itself upon one that scientific truth and human institutions do not satisfy any more. The reality of the opposites—good and evil, right and wrong, etc.—are inescapable. What then lies beyond? Is there some value that could transcend these opposites, a symbol that could embody them both and unite them once more? In other words, can the supreme value of wholeness that used to be experienced in relation to the parents be experienced again in a new and adult form?

And so we have to inquire what symbols can replace the powerful and valuable images of the Great Mother and the Spiritual Father when the hero has overcome the parents, and, beyond that, has overcome the parental images by taking upon himself the responsibility for his own life, as Ea and Marduk did when they overcame Apsu and Tiamat, the primal beings, and went on to establish law and order in the world. Modern young people have to do this too. When the hero departs on his own adventures, some of the energy he has wrested from the primal parents is invested in life, but what happens to that part—and it is by far the greater part—of the primal energy that remains with the archetype, the container of the immeasurable energy of the unconscious?

Up to this time the parental image has contained this *numinosum,* and obviously when the hero departs with his trophy he carries off a part of the parental hoard. But the hoard itself is hardly diminished by this "theft." It retreats into the further reaches of the unconscious, and is more remote from the hero, more inaccessible, than when he slept in the womb of the Mother and so felt identified with her.

In the Babylonian story, Apsu and Tiamat were overcome. For the purposes of the myth they had been represented first as fabulous monsters and then as human beings. They had been hypostatized—treated as if they were persons. So we hear of Apsu lying on a couch, taking Mummu on his knee, while Tiamat talks and gets angry and so on. As persons, they were killed by the hero. They were broken up, destroyed, and their powers were given to the lesser gods. But then they returned to their cosmic forms. The sacred shrine was built on the waters of Apsu, the Father, and while the laws of society were established with the power that had been wrested from him, Tiamat, the Mother, remained as she ever was. She cannot be destroyed. Her body forms the vault of heaven and the curve of the underworld. The whole world is thus encompassed within her sphere. She is a little less violent, a little less all-powerful than she was before, but she is the same old Tiamat and when the time comes she will arise, raging, to destroy her children and all their works—unless! Unless some new image, some new form, can be found in which the dynamism of the archetype can be contained. At some time in our personal lives we are all likely to be confronted with this problem. In fact, it is *the* great problem of humanity in the present stage of the world's history.

In *The Origins and History of Consciousness,* Erich Neumann points out that the hero who succeeds in splitting the archetypal image of the primal parents corresponds to the ego that has separated from the actual parents, and also from the unconscious itself, thus acquiring some part of the powerful contents of the unconscious for its own system, namely for consciousness. He writes:

> Fragmentation occurs in the sense that, for consciousness, the primordial archetype breaks down into a sizable group of related archetypes and symbols. Or rather, this group may be thought of as the periphery enclosing an unknown and intangible center.[63]

This stage of the hero exploit is shown in our myth, for when Marduk overcame Tiamat he immediately set up a pantheon of the gods and began to distribute the powers and fates among them. The contents of the unconscious, freed by the fragmentation of Tiamat, became the gods. One would have expected this settlement to be followed by a long period of peaceful development. But that is not what happened, for the gods were entirely unrelated to humanity, and al-

---

[63] *Origins*, p. 321.

though humanity was newly created, our presence became necessary at this point if the gods were to settle down peacefully, each in his shrine.

That people should become necessary at this point indicates that when the Mother is overcome and the emotions and drives are separated from each other, it is imperative that consciousness should be developed, otherwise everything will fall into chaos again. That is to say, the successful hero exploit does not lead to a time of slothful ease and the enjoyment of new freedom, untrammeled by parental controls. Quite the contrary. The new powers must immediately be set to work and this, in the myth, requires Man, with a capital M—that is, a greater consciousness than the ego alone can produce. This greater consciousness is the Anthropos, who will be able to embody the *image* of the gods or its psychological counterpart.

Apsu and Tiamat, the primal gods in our myth, were replaced by the pantheon of gods having qualities akin to those of their worshipers, and we find that gradually the gods became more human. They embodied attributes and powers that are nearer to our own, but on a heroic scale. Then another step was taken. The qualities of the gods were assimilated more or less into human consciousness, and humankind became more cultured, more disciplined, till the gods were finally depotentiated and gradually disappeared. Meanwhile, a new revelation from the unconscious, a new myth, arose and the numinous archetype clothed itself in the symbol of a Father God supreme over all. For many centuries this image was accepted as metaphysical truth. God was hypostatized, thought of as a concrete reality, but gradually the concept of God became more spiritual and appeared in less material guise. This was both a gain and a loss, since eventually for many people God's actual existence became quite problematic; as an agnostic once remarked, "God has become nothing but a gas," having lost all reality and power, but as a matter of fact the energy of the biggest atom bomb comes from hydrogen, which is also a gas.

In the meantime, the actual power of the archetype receded ever deeper into the unconscious, because the recognized symbols were no longer valid, or were not potent enough to mediate between humans and the numinous reality of the life-power. In the face of the unconscious, we were left protected and supported only by a pitifully inadequate ego. Consequently, the power of the collective unconscious is liable to break forth in chaotic form once more and, unless a new supreme symbol should arise to act as a mediator for the energies activated in the unconscious, it will prove to be destructive to our psyche and all our conscious works.

This is not the only consequence of the destruction of a religious symbol, for when there is no longer any symbol adequate to carry the value of a God-image, not only is conscious life deprived of a meaningful relation to the life forces, but the unconscious also seems to suffer. It becomes disturbed and its inner organization seems to dissolve, leaving in its stead a chaotic condition reminiscent of the rule of Apsu and Tiamat. This too can be considered an injury to the archetypal image.

I am making these statements as if this situation were a well-known and generally recognized fact that needs no proof. Naturally, since we are dealing with the unconscious, and the deep unconscious at that, there can be no *proof* of what happens or will happen, but of evidence there is a considerable amount. On the stage of history, for instance, the fall of the Roman Empire provides an example. When the gods had become merely figures in a narrative, divine power was thought to be embodied in the Caesar, a mere man, so that God came down to earth as a tyrant without moral or constitutional limits. Later, when the Caesar was overthrown, chaos followed. A similar sequence of events followed the denial of religion during the French Revolution. But if these historical examples are not enough to convince, we have ourselves recently witnessed what happens when a tyrant usurps the prerogatives of God and a totalitarian state is set up to replace all moral and religious allegiances. Then indeed it is as if the forces of Tiamat were let loose once more on the earth.

And what about the individual experience? When the parental rule has been overcome in what may be called the normal course of events, the son or daughter goes out into the world to fulfill his or her individual destiny. In this they are supported by the expectations and conventions of society and by their own instincts as well. And so the majority of men and women succeed in making an adjustment to the demands of outer life.

But can worldly success be taken as evidence that the primal parents have been overcome, in the psychological meaning of that term? Obviously in the outer sphere the children have become adults, but not all who seem to have made a satisfactory adaptation have actually done so, as any analyst could testify. Around the midpoint of life a satisfactory external adaptation may prove itself insufficient to meet the needs of the whole person. Repressed and forgotten sides of one's personality begin to clamor for recognition and a chance for life. And so the call comes from deep within oneself to undertake a new search, to explore new territory, where the objective will not be greater achievements in the outer world, but to find the repressed fragments of oneself and rescue the treasure hidden in the unconscious.

This is the task of individuation and the discovery of the treasure of the Self, or, in terms of *The Gospel of Truth,* referred to earlier, it is the Completeness of oneself. When humanity was led astray by Error we lost our Completeness, which remained with the Father. The writer of the *Gospel* tells us:

> The place where there is envy and quarreling is a Lack, but the place where is the Reunion is Completeness. For the lack arose because the Father was not known, but when the Father is known the Lack will not exist, from that moment. For the Lack is wont to melt away in the Completeness.[64]

The envy and quarreling that the text speaks of has to do with our unconsciousness of ourselves, so that we project our lack onto other people and blame them for our own defects. This exactly describes the condition of the son or daughter who blames the parents for his or her own psychological problems. Granted that the incompleteness of the parents has been instrumental in producing their child's lack, yet even so, as an adult one has to take upon oneself the task of finding one's completeness. We cannot put this responsibility upon anyone else. The above text says that when the Father is known, the Lack will melt away, because the knowledge of God is equivalent to the knowledge of oneself—they are inseparable. And in the Reunion—that is, of man with his split-off parts—"each one shall receive himself again."

In his commentary on this statement, Kendrick Grobel says:

> He who by the good news is made Gnostic (i.e., an enlightened one) receives two things, God and his own lost or forgotten self. Knowledge of God and of one's true self are two sides of the same thing; one cannot have one without the other.[65]

This receiving of one's "true self"—we would say the Self—*is* the Completeness, or in the terms of analytical psychology it is the "wholeness of the Self," which the text says remained with the Father when Error led humanity astray. This wholeness, according to *The Gospel of Truth,* is equivalent to coming to knowledge of the Father as he really is. In other words, an experience of the Self would mean a reconstruction of the God-image, formerly embodied in the archetypal images of the Great Mother and the Spiritual Father, which were fragmented through the development of ego-consciousness.

We will see how this works in the following chapter.

---

[64] *Gospel of Truth,* p. 66.
[65] Ibid., p. 68.

8
Reconstruction and Individuation

The call to embark on the task of reconstruction comes to many people at mid-life, when the outward thrust of libido is slowing down and success in the outer world begins to lose its paramount importance. Then the libido turns within, and if the inner life has remained on a childish level and one has lived psychologically in the world of illusion to which one was led by Error, things will begin to go wrong. One may become depressed, or symptoms of neurosis may develop.

The young person goes out into the world eager to create something new and unique. It is the "great adventure" and it captivates all one's libido. But gradually the creation itself begins to demand more and more energy, and the mature person becomes increasingly involved in responsibilities and the demands of that very thing created with such enthusiasm. Then, passing the crest of the hill and beginning to descend the other side—in the fifties, say—one feels bound to one's task, all freedom lost, ridden, even driven, by a self-made juggernaut. One sees no way to get free of responsibilities. The juggernaut may overtake one to the point of depression or a physical or mental breakdown.

Distresses of this kind constitute a call to undertake a radical reconstruction of the inner life. But there are other ways in which one may be called. The challenge to undertake this difficult task came to two people I know, one a man, the other a woman, each in a different way. In neither of them had the archetypal image of the Father or the Mother suffered a pathological injury through unfortunate childhood experiences. Nor did the depression into which each fell have any obvious outer cause. It was apparently just that the time had come when they were called upon to seek Completeness.

Most analysts have probably worked analytically with men and women who have made a satisfactory adjustment to life, only to fall into depression or some psychic conflict in middle or later life. If an investigation of the unconscious of such a person is undertaken, it will usually be found that one has not made as satisfactory an adaptation to the inner realm as one has to the outer. Or perhaps the adaptation was satisfactory for the years that are coming to a close, but one has been entirely oblivious of the fact that a new adaptation will be required for the latter half of life. Thus one continues to deal with life using an outworn model, as if one were trying to cope with the age of automobiles by riding a childhood bicycle—a rather common dream that many people have just at this point of transition.

The problem of what is the meaning and purpose of the second half of life becomes of chief concern in the analysis of older people. At the midpoint of life it becomes important, necessary even, to find a new symbol of value to act as mediator between the conscious elements of life and the numinous factors in the unconscious, one that will be adequate for oneself, individually. But this is not easy, for such people may feel that they have nothing within to hold on to. All the known values of life lose their reality, perhaps, or they develop fears and anxieties they have never known before, or that are so nebulous and fleeting that after a bad few minutes they are able to dismiss them. But these anxieties keep returning and will not be dismissed; chaos confronts one in dreams, or one finds oneself the victim of destructive powers whose nature and purpose is ominous. This is the kind of situation that Franz Kafka and other modern artists represent in their novels, and it is characteristic of an age that has lost its religion and its inner orientation.

A frequent characteristic of such experiences is the horror engendered by a sense of complete lack of order. In Bunyan's *Pilgrim's Progress* the Valley of the Shadow of Death is described as being covered with the clouds of confusion and utterly without order, which struck the travelers as peculiarly frightful. Dante too speaks of the chaos and lack of order in the realm of the Inferno. In such psychic states, a person seems to have become trapped in a place where God is not, where He does not exist. In other words, one has dropped into the chaos of the time before the beginning—and it is a dreadful experience. Jung says of it: "The primal experience is word- and imageless, for it is a vision in a 'dark mirror' . . . . It is like a whirlwind carrying everything before it."[66]

*

One night, just before Christmas, a man whom I shall call John dreamed that he had inherited a plot of land one foot square. In the dream he was engaged in planting a little spruce tree on it. He was told that this land and the tree would in turn be inherited by a child of his family, who was as yet unborn.

The foot-square plot of land associates to the foot-square house and the inch-square room that is used as a symbol of the house of the Self in *The Secret of the Golden Flower,* a Chinese text that Jung was very interested in.[67] The spruce tree was naturally connected with the Christmas Tree John had been decorating the evening before he had the dream. Traditionally, a Christmas tree has to be a spruce. The spruce is sacred to Dionysus in his role of Mystery God, the god of

---

[66] "Psychology and Poetry," pp. 19f.
[67] [See Richard Wilhelm, trans., *The Secret of the Golden Flower;* also "Commentary on 'The Secret of the Golden Flower,' " *Alchemical Studies,* CW 13, pars. 1ff.—Ed.]

emotion, ecstasy and the spirit of life. After having been slain and eaten by the Titans, Dionysus was born again, from Silene the Moon. A spruce tree grew up outside the cave where he was born, to protect him from being devoured by the Titans. So the spruce means the promise of the rebirth of the god of life, in his mystery form, that is, the god within. One can see why the spruce tree came to be used as the birth tree, not only celebrating the return of the sun, but also in celebration of the birth of Christ. This is the only birthday we celebrate for an infant who never, on Christmas Day in any event, gets any older. A human child's birthday keeps pace with chronological age, but that is not so with this birthday. It is always a celebration and re-evoking of the infant form of the god. It is the birth of a Mystery God.

One might expect that the dreamer would awake from such a dream with a feeling of joy and renewal. But when John awoke he had a very distressing experience. He wrote in his notebook:

Here I woke up, and as I reviewed the events of the dream I became very hot and felt as though I was suffocating. I gasped for breath and felt my chest would burst. Suddenly I became aware that I was surrounded by death and as though hell had risen up and swallowed me. It was a great void composed of hot dried mud, and it was everywhere, not only in me and surrounding me, like a suffocating prison, but extending to the farthest reaches of the cosmos.

Gradually I began to understand that this void, this death, was the ultimate reality, the foundation of all things and the groundwork of our illusory "life." Our life was really death after all. This filled me with horror and I tried to escape but I couldn't. I felt crucified between two impossibilities. I could neither live nor die. Both were equally horrible. All the while my chest felt as though it would burst. I was terrified and thought I might be going insane.

Vaguely I began to understand that the hot muddy void contained something tremendously alive and throbbing, the most powerful force in the universe. [At this point in his fantasy the dreamer is both in the mud and also outside it, observing the happening.] Yet this life force was imprisoned in death and suffocation. It cried out for release and seemed to say: "I am the Lord God and this is my condition, and the condition of everything in the universe."

This was the most horrible thing of all, to know that God himself was from the beginning and forever suffering a living death and in hell.

I sought frantically for some helpful thought or vision that would exorcise the deadly void. Then a voice spoke: "For once in your life you must face reality, and must do it *alone*. You must deal with it. You can do it. But you must fight with everything you've got."

Now I understood that the living thing inside the void was trying to come to life and expression through me.

Even after this, John still felt as though he were actually caught in that awful mud. This experience recurred at frequent intervals for about a month, not only at night but in the daytime as well.

So the first experience of the imminent birth of the Self is of being completely cut off from all companionship, human and divine, lost in a void, a chaos, in this case a chaos of mud, recalling the condition of the world before the creation, when it was without form. The mud was hot, just as the earth was hot in the beginning. The realization that within this muddy chaos there was someone with him—who John equates to the Lord God, a living, suffering spirit that cries out for release—recalls the alchemical vision of the King's Son who lies in the dark depths of the sea as though dead. But he yet lives and calls from the deep, "Whosoever will free me from the waters and lead me to dry land, him will I prosper with everlasting riches."[68] Or as another version has it:

> The earth hath been polluted and defiled in my works, for there was darkness over it because I stick fast in the mire of the deep and my substance is not disclosed. Wherefore out of the depths have I cried and from the abyss of the earth with my voice to all you that pass by the way. Attend and see me, if any shall find one like unto me, I will give into his hand the morning star.[69]

It is the as yet unrealized Self, equated by the alchemists to Christ, that is lost in the darkness of the unconscious. And John, in his experience, was told he must fight to recognize "reality," for that is the only thing that can release him. This is a very interesting statement. It corresponds to the passage from *The Gospel of Truth* where it is said that the return to our Completeness, that is, to the Self, will come about when we recognize the illusory quality of our view of the world and see the reality underlying it.

It is interesting to note that in the moment of greatest despair a "voice" came to John instructing him in what to do, just as in Nora's case a voice reassured her that it would remain within to advise her. John was an intuitive type, so his greatest struggle would be to accept reality. Nora's chief problem was that she had always taken the command of the animus as representing reality for her, hence the voice told her she must submit to the guidance of the Great Mother, that is, the feminine principle. In both cases it is the voice of God within, replacing the projected or hypostatized God without.

John's experience is not unique. The experience of being lost in the void is not unusual, preceding the coming to consciousness of the Self. One woman, Mary, dreamed she was floating in outer space with no means of orientation, no

---

[68] *Psychology and Alchemy,* CW 12, par. 434.

[69] Ibid., par. 434, note 33.

up or down, no forward or backward, no gravity, no direction, no starting-point, no goal. Life had become an unending, unrelated suspension. She too was filled with fear, terrorized by the fear of insanity. Both John and Mary were in the second half of life, and they had both made a satisfactory outer adaptation. There was no obvious reason why they should have been overtaken by such a devastating experience. But evidently the conscious order of their lives had become insufficient and in compensation they found themselves adrift, disoriented, face to face with an unordered, unknown emptiness, the void.

It is this void that one religion after another speaks of as "before the beginning"—that is, before consciousness has arisen. And it is this void that contains the *numinosum*, the energy that is the creative God-power. "In the beginning," we are told in the Bible, "the earth was without form, and void; and darkness was upon the face of the deep." (Gen. 1:1-2) The first act of creation was the coming of light, followed on the second day by the separation of the waters into those above and those below the firmament. For as Neumann says:

> The world begins only with the coming of light, which constellates the opposition between heaven and earth as the basic symbol of all other opposites. . . . With the rising of the sun or—in the language of ancient Egypt—the creation of the firmament, which divides the upper from the lower, mankind's day begins, and the universe becomes visible with all its contents.
>
> In relation to man and his ego, the creation of light and the birth of the sun are bound up with the separation of the World Parents and the positive and negative consequences which ensue for the hero who separates them.[70]

He continues later on:

> Space only came into being when, as the Egyptian myth puts it, the god of the air, Shu, parted the sky from the earth by stepping between them. [Similarly, Marduk divided Tiamat, the maternal abyss, into two parts by blowing the wind into her belly and so splitting her apart. The wind, of course, refers to the spirit.] Only then, as a result of his light-creating and space-creating intervention, was there heaven above and earth below, back and front, left and right—in other worlds, only then was space organized with reference to an ego.[71]

It is not possible to orient oneself in time and space until consciousness of the opposites has arisen; lacking that, one is lost in the void. Hence the terror felt by John and Mary was concerned more with a lack of orientation than with any actual threat of physical harm. Indeed, it is the very absence of any definite threat to life that makes the situation so terrifying. Death, in the sense of ending,

---

[70] *Origins*, pp. 106f.
[71] Ibid., p. 108.

would be welcome, but this was a living death, without beginning and without end. It represents, in fact, the obliteration of ego-consciousness. John had returned to the time before the beginning when there was no ego-consciousness at all. Such a condition, to one who has never developed an ego-consciousness, may constitute the bliss of the unborn babe. A person may sometimes experience such a feeling, akin to the euphoria produced by certain drugs, when one drifts off into the "empyrean" and loses all sense of reality and its obligations. But for an adult who has developed ego-consciousness and a sense of responsibility, to fall into such a condition spells the death of the ego, or insanity, unless out of this experience a new light might dawn, a new center of consciousness come into being, or, as our myth states it, unless Man, the Anthropos, could be created. And this, the myth declares, requires the blood of one of the gods. Kingu, son and spouse of the primal mother, Tiamat, was chosen for this role.

So, while in the first half of life the task is to emerge out of the darkness of total unconsciousness and develop an ego, in the second half the fate is to lose the hard-won ego-consciousness and experience once again the darkness of the first beginnings. This time, however, the loss of the ego must be accepted consciously, as a sacrifice. The fulfillment of the experience is the emergence not of an ego but of a new center of consciousness, one more nearly related to the archetype that had been overcome and fragmented during the hero-ordeal. The second experience of the void is not the same as the first. True, it precedes a coming to consciousness; not, however, to ego-consciousness—*that* had been achieved long ago. This time the experience comes as a temporary obliteration of the ego, corresponding to the fragmentation or death preceding initiation.

The consciousness that will arise out of the void, if all goes well, is *Self-consciousness*, corresponding to the creation of the Anthropos in our myth. That is, it is the "night-sea journey" with the birth of a new sun, corresponding to or symbolizing the resurrection of the initiated Egyptian as an Osiris, or it is the "wilderness" experience that results in the recognition of God as an inner presence, an inner voice in place of the hitherto hypostatized deity.

Let us go back to John's dream in which he was engulfed in black mud. This man was not sick, but he still had an unworked-out, or at least unresolved, problem with the mother archetype. He wanted a mother to love and care for him. And one might expect that he would have a vision of the Great Mother, especially as the dream that preceded the vision was connected with the Nativity. But, whatever he might have desired, the meaning of that dream is evidently not centered in the Mother but rather in the Child, the King of the time to come, for he was planting the spruce for an unborn child of his family whose inheritance it was to be.

The vision that followed immediately was of the void of hot mud, the motherless world. Yet in John's active imagination he discovered that he was not alone there. There was another with him, recalling the Biblical story of Shadrach, Meshach and Abednego thrown into the fiery furnace by order of Nebuchadnezzar. (Dan. 3) And this "other" cried out for release, a release that must be achieved through the dreamer's effort. The companion was not the Great Mother who might take care of the situation, but rather one who needs *his* help.

John's dream and the persistent fantasy that followed it, pursuing him, as it did, for almost a month, was so disturbing that he attempted to draw the situation, though it seemed a rather impossible task because the horror of the dream was largely due to the fact that the experience had no boundaries, either of time or space. So how could he confine it to a piece of paper and fasten it, as it were, to present time and to the three dimensions? It took a good deal of concentration to accomplish this, as the mud always tried to escape the bounds he set for it, just as Tiamat sought to escape Marduk's net. But when at last he succeeded in capturing the experience sufficiently clearly to make a drawing of it, he found that the mud had become confined within a circle, as is shown in the picture (Figure 16). His anguish, too, is clearly portrayed as is his helplessness. Interestingly enough, he is shown as primitive, animal-like.

Figure 16

But one thing that he had not intended appeared in the picture—the *eye*. This must mean that the mud itself has begun to have a glimmer of consciousness—or, more accurately, the dreamer begins "unconsciously" to see. In the active imagination before he drew the picture, this emerging consciousness, this understanding, was expressed as the voice of the Lord God. In the alchemical text cited above in amplification of this point, God would be represented by the King, and the King's Son would be equivalent to Christ, or it would be an *imago Christi,* an image of Christ. The alchemist would call this the Royal Son.

The idea of the Christ is obviously connected with the spruce tree John had planted in his dream, and it is also related to the Christmas tree he and his wife had been decorating the previous evening. So the tree is here a symbol of the Self, just as it is in the Dionysian myth, where it represents the god in his mystery form. It is in the form of this spirit-tree that the god possessed the initiates, thus being incarnate in them. The King's Son lost in the darkness of the muddy sea would, in analytical terms, represent the Christ-image within the darkness of the unconscious psyche—that is, it is an image of the Self that is as yet not realized. And so we may say that the eye belongs to the Self.

The eye is at once the eye of God and the eye of consciousness in the unconscious.[72] Not only does it bring the possibility of escape from his own torment, but it promises release for the King's Son (that is, the Self), who is also in torment. And indeed, this is shown by what happened next, for he escaped through the eye, as may be seen in the next picture (Figure 17). And, as a matter of fact, John was not troubled again by the sense of being imprisoned in the mud. His claustrophobia did not return.

A glance at the figure that escapes from the mud, as it were, born out of the eye, will show that an amazing change has taken place in his appearance. It is as if he had indeed been reborn and is now a new man. He is no longer an almost ape-like creature. He is still primitive, but now he is definitely human and he is no longer in agony.

The woman Mary, who had dreamed that she was floating in outer space, also tried to draw, not the actual dream but a fantasy of the *monad,* the unity of the total human being—the microcosm of man—as she experienced it. Interestingly enough, though she knew nothing of mandalas or the like, she too drew a sphere (Figure 18). In her case it did not consist of mud, representing the earth, but

---

[72] [For further elucidation of the psychological significence of the eye in dreams and drawings, see Edward F. Edinger, *The Creation of Consciousness: Jung's Myth for Modern Man,* pp. 42ff.; also Edinger, *The Mysterium Lectures: A Journey through Jung's Mysterium Coniunctionis,* pp. 63ff., 218f.—Ed.]

Figure 17

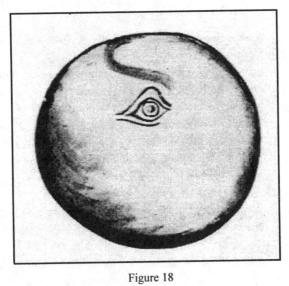

Figure 18

of air, which would represent the sky or the heavens, which corresponds to the form of the dream, in which she was floating in outer space. And she, too, found, rather to her surprise, that she had given her sphere an eye. She said: "The eye is that which sees and also that which reveals." She at once associated it to the eye of God, meaning that it represented a not-personal, or suprapersonal, consciousness that belongs to the *monad* as the totality of both conscious and unconscious.

John had had a good deal of difficulty in making the circle to enclose or confine the muddy void. But eventually he did. So much for the drawing. But what psychological entity could the circle symbolize? What human power might be able to contain or enclose the unconquered part of the archetypal energy? What could it possibly be made of? In order to get even a hint of an answer to these questions, we must turn again for guidance to the mythologems that deal with this aspect of the human problem.

Neumann points out that when the hero has overcome the containing mother-father world and broken out of his imprisonment in the parental uroboros, he takes with him some part of its energy, and with this he builds his world. He goes on to say that the fragments of the dismembered primal archetype form a group of related archetypes. These "lesser archetypes" are, of course, represented in the Babylonian myth by the company of gods, among whom Marduk distributed the powers he had wrested from the primal potencies, Apsu and Tiamat. These secondary archetypes, according to Neumann, then form a protective circle that encloses the remaining energies of the primal archetype, a center which persists as an unknown and intangible center of immeasurable dynamism. This is a most important concept, but it is couched in such condensed language that its significance can easily be overlooked.

In other words, Neumann states that as a result of the hero battle the primal archetype, the *numinosum,* is surrounded by secondary archetypes. That is to say, a person first experiences or exists in a totality, a wholeness—in the All—which means in God, or in the uroboros. Then, through the development and education of the individual, the archetypes are split off from the All. These represent aspects of the unknowable divine *numinosum* that can be experienced by the human being, at least in symbol form. These, like the gods of our myth, then surround the unknowable *numinosum,* shielding the individual from the potentially devastating experience of the Living God. It is like the Jewish formulation of the *En Soph,* emanating the ten Sephirot that represent and conceal the real essence of the ineffable.

The archetypal images of the culture we have been born into, and the symbols of our religion, function in exactly the same way. This corresponds in the symbolism of our myth to the establishment by Marduk of the planetary gods, who represent our emotional and instinctive urges and exert such a powerful influence on our fate. In antiquity the planets were thought to circle the world. Their orbits represented their spheres of influence or power, while the not-personal, the deeper unconscious part of the psyche, was still represented by Tiamat and Apsu. The planetary gods thus formed a protective circle round the still unexplored primal archetype, so that its numinous and fearsome energy could not impinge directly on humanity and threaten our sanity.

The gods were lonely, however, and could not satisfy their own hunger, so Man was created to serve the gods and bring them sacrifices. In this way it was hoped that they might be content to reside each in his own sphere and not fall to quarreling with neighboring gods. So we see that at a certain point in the development of human life consciousness became necessary, and in the myth consciousness was represented by Man. The service of the gods and the sacrifices made to them correspond not only to religious observances, but also to acceptance of the conventions of culture, by which the gods of anger, hate and lust are appeased and kept each in their own sphere, so that the human world shall not be devastated by their unmitigated violence. This, of course, represents the normal course of development and, when things go well and there is no disturbance in the unconscious, these rules serve to order the human world.

However, when the rituals and symbols of religion, or the mores that control collective behavior, have broken down, the old forms may prove ineffective and the untamed forces of instinctive life may break through into consciousness with devastating results. On the level of the individual, where there has been no adequate carrier for the numinous archetypal symbol, and because of an unfortunate childhood situation the person has had no satisfactory mother or father experience, or where, perhaps, the parents have been inadequate carriers of the archetypal parental image in its positive form, a pathological injury of the archetypal image results. When a person suffering from such a condition goes into analysis, the task with which both analyst and analysand are confronted is to further, as much as possible, the reconstruction of the injured archetypal image, in the hope that there may arise a symbol that is both acceptable to consciousness and powerful enough to represent the archetype.

The first stage of analysis in such a case is usually concerned, as it was with Nora, with the release of the person from a negative attitude toward the parents and the parental image, through the projection of a positive parental image onto the analyst. When this has occurred and has been accepted, with all the emotions such a change involves, the analysand can proceed with his or her life on an entirely new basis.

But in John and Mary, the two whose dreams were presented above, there had been no such injury to the archetypal image. Indeed, each had made a satisfactory adaptation to life. It was only when they reached their forties that they encountered the experience of the void that so disturbed them. These were numinous experiences that demanded attention.

There are various ways of dealing with such experiences. St. Nicholas von der Flüe, popularly known as Brother Klaus, found one way. Jung reminds us that the vision Brother Klaus had of the awe-ful face of God was so horrible that his own countenance was changed by it.[73] Those who saw Brother Klaus were terrified of him and he himself said that he feared his heart would burst in pieces—that is to say, he feared he would suffer psychic disintegration. He devoted long years of concentrated attention to understanding his vision, and only after this labor of assimilation was the balance of his psyche restored. So, too, in the cases of John and Mary, much work was needed before a new symbol or archetypal image, adequate to bear the burden of life, could be developed.

Brother Klaus took his disturbing image with him into the *temenos* of his monastic cell, which acted like an incubation chamber. Similar cells were used in antiquity for the treatment of insanity. The shrines of Asclepius, the god of healing of ancient Greece, for instance, had such cells where the afflicted slept close to the image of the god which, like the Apsu temple of the Babylonians, was placed over a spring, source of the life-giving waters, the sap of life. While the patient slept and the conscious mind was put to rest, the person's unconscious was laid open to the influence of the god. In this way it was believed that a healing symbol of reconciliation might arise in one's dreams.

The analytic situation can be like an incubation chamber. The person experiencing psychic distress tells the analyst about it, and the analyst's attitude of acceptance often has a quieting effect on the unconscious, so that the sufferer is enabled to look at dreams and other unconscious material with less resistance. This makes for a helpful psychic atmosphere in which the healing symbol may be found.

The ancients sought to restore the sufferer to health under the symbol of the particular god in whose temple healing rites were performed, just as Brother Klaus sought to assimilate his vision within the framework of the Christian Church. Analysis has no such dogmatic formulation, whose teaching might carry the healing image. Rather, the effective symbol in the analytic situation must come as a personal experience and achievement; the archetypal God-image must be replaced by the image of the god within. The new apprehension of God must

---

[73] [See "Brother Klaus," *Psychology and Religion*, CW 11, pars. 474ff.—Ed.]

be approached and comprehended through the experience of the Self, which Jung has shown by many examples to have the value of an inner God-image. Or, to use the symbolism of our Babylonian myth, the value that can stand vis-à-vis the gods is not the personal ego but the Anthropos, an equivalent of the Self.

In John's case, where the experience of the void came as a dream of being imprisoned in black mud, the first step in the resolution of his psychic distress was represented as the emergence—the birth, really—of a new man through the eye. This would mean that his new attitude was connected with greater insight, greater understanding, than he had previously possessed. Since the eye was associated by him with the eye of God, this new insight would be as if he saw from a new point of view. It would not be a bird's-eye view, but, so to say, a God's-eye view—an attitude sometimes spoken of as viewing things *sub specie aeternitatis*.

It was some time after this, when many interesting things had occurred in John's analysis, that the theme of rebirth came up again. But even at this stage, a great change had taken place. The symbol for what was reborn changed in a remarkable way, for he dreamed that a light figure with flaming hair and carrying a sword emerged from a cornucopia with a flash of lightning (Figure 19). John called this figure Ariel.

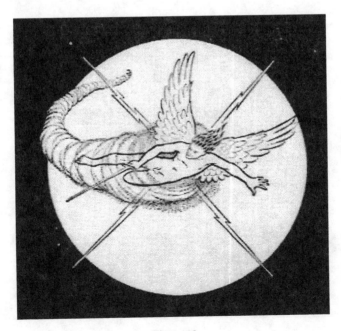

Figure 19

Ariel is an equivalent of the alchemical Mercurius, and for a modern person has reverberations from Shakespeare's *The Tempest,* where Ariel is the bright spirit of Prospero, his spiritual self. In John's drawing Ariel is seen born from the cornucopia, so that his appearance presages the coming of great wealth—not in terms of money, of course, but a wealth of life energy, libido, just as the alchemists' quest was for gold which they called "*our* gold, not *vulgar* gold," meaning that their gold represented spiritual value rather than material wealth.

But this was still only the beginning of the resolution of John's problem, a foreshadowing of a possible outcome. For on the anniversary of the dream of the mud—that is, on Christmas Day of the following year—he dreamed he saw a group of primitives sitting around a fire. They were singing and laughing. In particular he noticed one man who seemed to be having an especially happy time (Figure 20). John woke up and drew this happy, natural man, but only then did he notice, much to his surprise, that although the man resembled the original man in the mud, he was quite changed. No longer was he in distress, nor was he nearly so primitive. As he was thinking about this dream and contemplating the picture he had made, John saw an eye above and to the right of the fire which was not actually in the dream, nor was it in his drawing. It was a sort of vision, and as he looked at the eye it began to move toward him. It continued to move

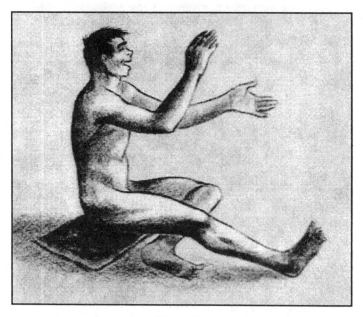

Figure 20

till it reached his body. Then silently it slipped inside his chest and came to rest in his heart, leaving him with an almost physical sense of well-being and joy.

During the year that had passed since that first dream with its disturbing claustrophobia, a considerable change had taken place in John's conscious condition. No longer was he somewhat out of touch with reality and the demands of daily life. He had experienced a renewal of energy and interest. He had evidently made progress on a deeper level as well, for the unconscious now represents his condition by this primitive man, who looks anything but depressed. It is as though the instinctive energies were alive again, perhaps as they had never been for him before.

This material has another feature that recalls the first picture he drew containing the eye (Figure 16, page 135). In that earlier vision the eye was interpreted as a symbol of a consciousness that transcends the consciousness of the ego, and in addition it represented the Self. In his new vision, the eye, symbol of the new consciousness, enters him and takes up its place in his heart. In my experience this is true: the Self first comes into consciousness not in the mind but in the heart. This fact is recognized in common parlance when we speak, for instance, of "the heart of the matter." And in the Tantric scheme of the levels of consciousness developed through yoga, the Purusha, or Lord—the indwelling God—first appears in the heart region, where he is represented by a small flame, an inner light by which one can see. It is only when the feeling of the heart is aroused, or enlightened, that one can really become conscious of oneself and of others as separate beings.

So long as our consciousness of others and our feeling for them is dependent on the value they have for us—whether positive or negative—we are not really conscious of them as persons in their own right. It is only when consciousness arises in the heart that we can be aware of them as separate individuals. In the language of Tantric Buddhism, when the Purusha appears in the heart region a tiny light is lit there. In psychological terms it would mean that when the Self arises in the heart, then a new kind of consciousness is born. It is by this light that we are enabled to see things *as they are.* When we are guided by this light, our actions and reactions will have a validity they lacked before.

Shortly after he had this dream, John's wife was stricken with a fatal illness. She lingered on for some months and died the following December. They had been very close. Her death brought him great sorrow and left him feeling desolate and terribly lonely. Then, about six months later, the night before his birthday, he dreamed again. He wrote:

> This is my birthday and I woke up remembering a dream fragment I'd had. The scene of the dream was a great mud hole, and the mud was moist and warm. A

group of kindly people immersed me in the mud up to my chest. Then they helped me out. When I came out of the mud-bath, the mud clung to me, weighing me down somewhat, but giving me a feeling of stability and security.

John felt this to be both an initiation and a rebirth.

The mud recalls that first vision of the mud-void in which he and the primitive man were trapped. At that time the condition seemed to be entirely negative—an experience of the "dark night of the soul." Here the feeling of the dream has changed fundamentally. The immersion in the mud obviously represents a sort of baptism, an initiation ceremony. In the first dream John's isolation was a particularly distressing element. This time he is not alone, but is helped by a group of kindly people. He is evidently being initiated into some sort of community, as postulants are initiated into secret societies or into mystery cults. Unless such initiations have become entirely banal, they have a numinous quality and usually a religious significance.

Christian baptism is represented as a rebirth or as a birth of the soul, so in this case, too, the emergence from the bath is a rebirth. Here, however, the medium is not water but mud. In the first dream the mud was hot; now its temperature is modified, so that the intense heat that connected the experience with the conventional idea of Hell is absent. The heat of Hell represents unbridled passions, so the warmth of the mud in this dream likely refers to feeling. After his immersion the mud clung to the dreamer, giving him a sense of security, which means that he has now been initiated into the earthly realm. In psychological terms it is an initiation on the sensation side, and this gives him both security and weight. Recall that in the first dream series, the task imposed on him by the voice was that he must find a means by which he could face reality.

John commented on the dream as follows:

The bath gave me a feeling of heaviness and a comfortable sense of security. I felt at home with myself. The comfortable feeling stayed with me for several days. Then one day I saw myself outside the mud hole, clothed only in trousers of mud, with muddy hands and feet [Figure 21]. In this condition I went to my office, going about my usual work. Then it dawned on me that I must be identified with the mud and was probably inflated. The drawing shows the moment of becoming aware of this condition.

Then I became dissatisfied and recalled the original dream image to see what would happen. It seemed to me that something was missing. Half of me was being bathed in mud. The other half needed a bath too. Then it began to rain and I said, "This is better." But as I watched the rain coming down I became afraid that the fire in my heart would be extinguished. A ring of fire appeared and circled around my chest as a protection [Figure 22]. Then the vision faded.

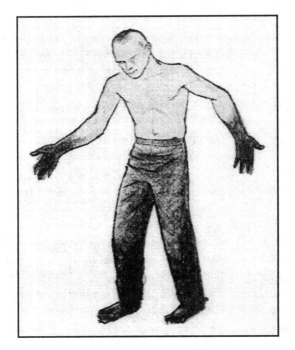

Figure 21

Figure 22

The fire in this man's heart relates to the light of the Purusha that had been kindled in his heart by the entry of the eye in the earlier vision. The circle of fire around his chest recalls the "circling of the light" that Chinese yoga tells of, resulting from the successful performance of yogic disciplines. And so we can say with some certainty that a transformation of the instincts has been achieved up to the level of the heart region.

In the case of Mary, the woman who found herself suspended in outer space, the resolution of her problem came in a different form. She dreamed one night that she went to her analytic hour and found that instead of the analyst a large star was enthroned in the analyst's chair (Figure 23). This sounds incongruous and somewhat absurd, but when it is remembered that the analyst's chair represents the analytic relationship, it does not seem so ridiculous.

It is in the actual encounter with the analyst during the analytic hour that the two worlds of the analysand come together. In dreams and fantasies, the analysand is alone—terribly alone. In the outer world, outside the consulting room, one is also alone, for the weight of subjective experience cuts one off from any real relation with people. We feel that no one could possibly understand what we are going through, and that if we tried to tell them they would think us crazy.

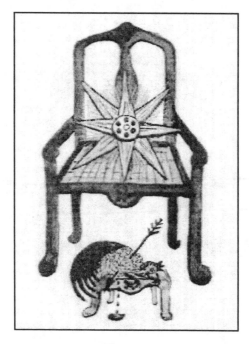

Figure 23

So we conceal our most intense experiences from others. But in the analytic relationship we are able to reveal at least a part of our inner life, either in words or
in pictures and through our dreams. By what seems almost like a miracle the
analyst has understood and respected our most secret thoughts. In the consulting
room one has found a *temenos,* a sacred enclosure, where one can be entirely
frank and unafraid of being misunderstood.

For Mary this was a most important experience. Her inner life had been intense and of the greatest importance to her, but never before had she been able to
talk about it with anyone. So it is not surprising that she developed a very strong
transference onto me, her analyst. The realization of her feelings came to her
one day and produced considerable conflict. In one part of herself she knew that
she did not want to have an affair with the analyst, that she was not in love with
this human being, and yet she was possessed by strong loving feelings.

It was then that she dreamed of going to her analytic hour, knowing that she
would have to acknowledge her feelings and dreading the encounter, only to
find in her dream that the analyst's chair was occupied not by the analyst but by
the large golden star. In her dream a dead cock lay on a footstool before the
chair. When she awoke, she drew the experience as she had seen it in her dream.
The analyst, who in real life occupied the chair, had been replaced by a star,
symbol of wholeness and, to Mary, also a symbol of the Self because she was
familiar with the idea that we are each born under a star that represents our individual fate and character.

So the dream says, in effect: "Your intense feelings are not for the person of
the analyst, but for the individual value she represents for you." This is what
accounts for the feelings of awe and reverence that were a part of her love. This
element of reverence is also hinted at in her drawing, for the chair she drew was
not my actual chair, but associated to a bishop's chair that had appeared in an
earlier dream.

The dream is particularly instructive because it points up the two aspects, two
dimensions, of the analytic situation. Mary's intense emotion was constellated
by the occupant of the analyst's chair, but the dream points out to her: "This is
your own individual value, not the person of the analyst. The analyst is only the
carrier of the value represented by the star. She is the mediator between you and
the numinous archetype, and so the dream brings you a reconciling symbol."
This is the personal aspect of the transference, but the personal aspect was also
necessary. If Mary had not been willing to accept her emotions in spite of the
conflict this involved, the healing could not have occurred. It was only because
she was able, as a result of the dream, to recognize, at one and the same time,
both the actual human situation and the subjective and transpersonal one, that a

reconciliation of these apparently incompatible elements could be accomplished in the star, symbol of the Self and of wholeness. It was the recognition of this differentiation that led to healing. It was an insight of the heart as well as of the head. Thus Mary was no longer so dependent on her analyst; she would not suffer a so-called transference neurosis.

In the dream her immunity is paid for, as it were, by the sacrifice of a cock. Mary associated the cock to the scene at the death of Socrates, where he enjoined his friend to sacrifice a cock for him to Asclepius. By this Socrates implied that by his death he was healed of the disease of mortality. The conflict within him between the earthly and spiritual parts of himself was resolved. He became whole.

Mary's conflict corresponds to the situation Socrates was confronted with. In her, too, the earthly, or carnal, and the spiritual, or psychological, elements were at war, evidenced by her conflicting feelings for her analyst. But the realization that the compelling attraction she felt for her analyst covered and concealed her yearning for wholeness brought healing. Her desire for a mutual love relationship with this other human being contained carnal longings which had to be sacrificed in order to find the real meaning of the experience. This is symbolized by the sacrifice of the cock, for in Hindu symbolism the cock represents lust. However, the cock is also the herald of a new day, and through the acceptance of the star as a symbol of wholeness, a new day dawned for Mary.

In this case the healing function of the analytic situation is clearly demonstrated. The analytic chair served as a symbol of the dual nature of the relationship between analysand and analyst, corresponding to the dual nature of humankind—the personal and the not-personal. That is, it brings into focus the relation between the ego and the Self.

In our understanding of the nature and function of the analytic relationship, it is most important that we make a clear distinction between these two parts. If we do not do so, the analysis itself will be severely damaged and the outcome will be jeopardized. There is first the human part, which must not be minimized since it represents the analysand's relation to external life. In the beginning, personal feelings and reactions may have to be kept in the background in the interests of the therapy, but eventually they must be recognized and allowed for by both parties. But by far the most important part of the relationship is what is usually called transference, because it consists of emotional reactions to projected material that the analyst carries for the analysand until it can be understood and assimilated by the latter. When this time comes, the analyst is relieved of the burden of the unrecognized psychic contents of the analysand. But, in the meantime, as the relation between the two persons has come about for psychotherapeutic reasons, this aspect of the relationship must take precedence over all other considerations. The "purpose" of the whole relationship is concealed in the transference, by means of which, if the situation is favorable, the patient can reconcile the warring elements within that caused the original difficulty.

We have wandered a long way from our myth, where we left the primal gods wounded, defeated and despoiled by the heroic enterprise of Marduk, who, while being a son of the gods, born in the sacred Apsu, yet showed human characteristics and performed the task of creating humans and ordering the world for their occupancy. Apsu had already been subdued in some measure by his father, Ea, who had set up his shrine on the waters of the Abyss. This shrine became the sacred place where the gods were worshiped. So out of Ea's victory a new relation to the masculine principle was established and the religious service of the gods was developed. A reconciliation had taken place between men and the masculine gods. In this way the masculine aspect of the original chaos was brought into relation to humankind.

But Tiamat, the feminine Abyss, who had been split wide open by Marduk's attack, had vanished from the scene. She remained inaccessible, unaccountable, dangerous and also necessary to life, for from her alone came the power to produce new life, to bear children, and to nourish life on earth. She was the source of the emotions and, to this day, as we know very well, this is the aspect of life that has remained the most uncontrollable and capricious, the most prone to drive us into destructive outbreaks that do not accord at all with our more civilized and disciplined masculine way.

Due to the phenomenon of the transference, the most uncontrollable emotions may be experienced within the safe enclosure of the analytic situation. In Mary's dream this was symbolized by the analytic chair and the realization that the projected emotions did not belong to the analyst but to the Self, represented in her case by a star. In this way the values that were formerly experienced by the analysand as if they were characteristics of the analyst, are assimilated, not by the ego but by one's not-personal core, the Self.

This is perhaps what is mean by these sayings of Jesus recorded in *The Gospel According to Thomas:*

> Jesus said: When you see your likeness, you rejoice. But when you see your images which came into existence before you, (which) neither die nor are manifested, how much will you bear![74]

---

[74] A. Guillaumont et al., trans., *The Gospel According to Thomas*, p. 17. (This is one of the codices discovered at Nag Hamadi in Egypt in 1945.)

And:

When you make eyes in the place of an eye, and a hand in the place of a hand, and a foot in the place of a foot, (and) an image in the place of an image, then shall you enter [the kingdom].[75]

The first saying asks: "How can you bear to see your real Self?" And the second says: "In the place of the outer form, make an inner image—then you shall enter the kingdom." Now this is exactly what Mary's dream also shows, namely that the outer image of the analyst must be replaced by its reality—the image, or symbol, of the Self.

In analysis the recognition of the Self emerges as a result of distinguishing between the archetypal and the personal parts of the relation to the analyst, which brings about a corresponding differentiation between the Self and the ego. This distinction between the human and the suprahuman, or to speak in mythological terms, between the human and the divine parts of the human being, is of the utmost importance. Without it, the experiences we have touched on would produce a dangerous inflation, with all the unfortunate consequences this condition brings. When one is inflated one flies away from the earth. As Nora's dream put it: the man who could fly to the moon and back in three and a half hours would be out of touch with the ground. Such an inflation inevitably results in separation from reality; it would produce isolation in outer life and also a return to the terrible experience of the void in the inner realm—that is, alienation from the reality of one's psychic life.

The danger of identifying with the archetype of the Self, which inevitably results in inflation, is especially great when the parental image is badly damaged. In such cases there is no experience from childhood that could serve as a mediator between the two worlds. Those whose relation to the parents has been unsatisfactory have a profound distrust of anyone in the role of parent. They cannot credit that the disinterested concern of the analyst is real, and so cannot freely give themselves in relation to the analyst, which really means to give oneself to the value that the analyst represents. When this is so, should the reconciling symbol be glimpsed in dreams as a result of the analytic work, it will only dissolve again into the chaos out of which it emerged. But when a conscious subjective experience is made real—which usually requires the inclusion of the analyst in a true confrontation, an *Auseinandersetzung*—the analysand discerns and realizes ("makes real") the distinction between the ego and the Self.

An experience of this kind brings healing to the injured archetypal image, as

---

[75] Ibid., p. 19.

well as to the suffering human being, for the symbol of the Self, of wholeness, is able to confront its opposite, chaos, without disintegrating. They are in a sense equal opposites, and the powers of the unknown are mediated once more to humankind through just this symbol. But while the image of the Self may be glimpsed through such experiences as we have been examining, only a fragment of its numinous power is lived in actuality; our human ability to realize it is by no means adequate to the task. By far the greater part of the *numinosum* recedes once more into the depths of the unconscious where, as it is said in *The Gospel According to St. Thomas:*

> The images are manifest to man and the Light which is within them is hidden in the Image of the Light of the Father. He will manifest himself and His Image is concealed by His Light.

Just as in primitive society the king is truly a mediator between humanity and the gods, being human in his manhood but divine in his kingship, so this realization of the Self within the psyche not only informs and guides personal life, it also acts as mediator between consciousness and the numinous potencies of the unconscious. In this way, calm begins to replace the war and chaos that were stirred up in the depths by the destruction of the archetypal parental image in its positive form. Order begins to be manifested once more in those deeper layers of the unconscious that had been activated by the revolt of ego-consciousness, and a new image of the archetype emerges—one mediated by the symbol of the Self. Thus the injury to the archetypal image is healed and there is peace once more between heaven and earth.

The foregoing had gone to press when I received a letter from John telling me that he had had what he called "the final dream of the series." He dreamed that he saw a rosebush whose flower was a tiny baby, and a voice said, "So your wife had a child after all!" "By this," he wrote, "I understood that I must be the father of the child." The child reminded him of the first dream where it was said that the square plot of land and the spruce tree he planted on it would be inherited by "a child of his family, as yet unborn."

And so the dream series that started six years before with a promise was now fulfilled. The miraculous child born in the rosebush, as well as being the child of himself and his inner wife—that is, his anima—is a symbol of the Self, the hero-child, that gradually emerged into consciousness as a result of all the work John had done on himself.

Bibliography

Adler, Gerhard. *The Living Symbol* (Bollingen Series LXIII). New York: Pantheon Books, 1961.

_____, ed. *Current Trends in Analytical Psychology: Proceedings of the First International Congress for Analytical Psychology.* London: Tavistock, 1961.

Arnold, Matthew. *Selected Poems.* Ed. Timothy Peltason. New York: Penguin Classics, 1995.

Bond, D. Stephenson. *The Archetype of Renewal: Psychological Reflections on the Aging, Death and Rebirth of the King.* Toronto: Inner City Books, 2003.

Campbell, Joseph. *The Hero with a Thousand Faces* (Bollingen Series XVII). Princeton: Princeton University Press, 1949.

Edinger, Edward F. *The Bible and the Psyche: Individuation Symbolism in the Old Testament.* Toronto: Inner City Books, 1986.

_____. *The Creation of Consciousness: Jung's Myth for Modern Man.* Toronto: Inner City Books, 1984.

_____. *Ego and Archetype: Individuation and the Religious Function of the Psyche.* New York: Penguin, 1973.

_____. *Encounter with the Self: A Jungian Commentary on William Blake's* Illustrations of the Book of Job. Toronto: Inner City Books, 1986.

_____. *The Mysterium Lectures: A Journey through Jung's* Mysterium Coniunctionis. Toronto: Inner City Books, 1995.

_____. *Transformation of the God-Image: An Elucidation of Jung's* Answer to Job. Toronto: Inner City Books, 1994.

Fierz-David, Linda. *Women's Dionysian Initiation: The Villa of Mysteries in Pompeii.* Putnam, CT: Spring Publications, 2001.

Grobel, Kendrick, trans. *The Gospel of Truth.* New York: Abingdon Press, 1959.

Guillaumont, A., et al., trans. *The Gospel According to Thomas.* New York: Harper & Brothers, 1959.

Harding, M. Esther. *The I and the Not-I* (Bollingen Series X). Princeton: Princeton University Press, 1974.

_____. *The Way of All Women: A Psychological Interpretation.* Boston: Shambhala Publications, 2001.

_____. *Woman's Mysteries: Ancient and Modern.* Boston: Shambhala Publications, 2001.

The I Ching or Book of Changes. Trans. Richard Wilhelm. London: Routledge & Kegan Paul Ltd., 1974.

Jacobi, Jolande. *Complex/Archetype/Symbol in the Psychology of C.G. Jung.* New York: Bollingen, 1971.

Jung, C.G. *C.G. Jung Letters* (Bollingen Series XCV). 2 vols. Ed. Gerhard Adler and Aniela Jaffé. Princeton: Princeton University Press, 1973.

_____. *The Collected Works* (Bollingen Series XX). 20 vols. Trans. R.F.C. Hull. Ed. H. Read, M. Fordham, G. Adler, Wm. McGuire. Princeton: Princeton University Press, 1953-1979.

_____. *Memories, Dreams, Reflections.* Ed. Aniela Jaffé. Trans. Richard and Clara Winston. New York: Vintage, 1989.

_____. "Psychology and Poetry." Trans. Eugene Jolas. In *Transitions: An International Quarterly for Creative Experiment,* June 1930.

Kierkegaard, Søren. *The Sickness unto Death.* Princeton: Princeton Univerzity Press, 1983.

Langdon, Stephen Herbert. *Semitic.* Vol. 5 of *The Mythology of All Races.* Ed. J.A. Macculloch and G.F. Moore. New York: Macmillan, 1931.

McGuire, William, and Hull, R.F.C., eds. *C.G. Jung Speaking: Interviews and Encounters* (Bollingen Series XCVII). Princeton: Princeton University Press, 1977.

Neumann, Erich. *Amor and Psyche.* Princeton: Princeton University Press, 1971.

_____. *The Great Mother* (Bollingen Series XLVII). Princeton: Princeton University Press, 1972.

_____. *The Origins and History of Consciousness* (Bollingen Series XLII). Princeton: Princeton University Press, 1970.

Otto, Rudolf. *The Idea of the Holy.* Trans. John W. Harvey. London: Oxford University Press, 1958.

Perera, Sylvia Brinton. *Descent to the Goddess: A Way of Initiation for Women.* Toronto: Inner City Books, 1981.

Rogers, Robert Williams. *The Religion of Babylonia and Assyria.* New York: Eaton and Mains, 1908.

Sharp, Daryl. *Digesting Jung: Food for the Journey.* Toronto: Inner City Books, 2001.

_____. *Jung Lexicon: A Primer of Terms and Concepts.* Toronto: Inner City Books, 1991.

_____. *Jungian Psychology Unplugged: My Life As an Elephant.* Toronto: Inner City Books, 1998.

_____. *Personality Types: Jung's Model of Typology.* Toronto: Inner City Books, 1987.

_____. *The Survival Papers: Anatomy of a Midlife Crisis.* Toronto: Inner City Books, 1988.

Smith, Sidney. *The Babylonian Legends of the Creation and the Fight between Bel and the Dragon as Told by Assyrian Tablets from Nineveh.* London: The British Museum, 1931.

Toynbee, Arnold. *A Study of History.* Oxford, UK: Oxford University Press, 1987.

von Franz, Marie-Louise. *The Problem of the Puer Aeternus.* Toronto: Inner City Books, 2000.

Wilhelm, Richard, trans. *The Secret of the Golden Flower.* London: Kegan Paul, 1931.

Index

Page nos. in *italic* refer to illustrations.

conscious(ness), 11-12, 16, 20, 28-31, 35,
    40, 45, 52, 56, 62, 68-69, 74-75, 78-
    79, 89, 113, 121-122, 126-127, 130,
    134, 139, 143, 151
  and conflict with unconscious, 16, 56, 69
  development of, 21, 44, 46, 80-88, 128
  evolution of, 95
  within the unconscious, 43, 136
creation myth(s), 29, 95, 133
  Babylonian, 25-28, 32-55, 89, 125-126,
    134, 138-139, 149
Cronos, 27

dark and light, 58
death, dream of acceptance of, 106
decisive question, 17
Demeter and Kore, 120
dependence, 94, 96
depression, 85, 88, 90, 129
Dionysian/Dionysus, 28, 36, 130-131, 136
disobedience, 83
double fatherhood, 55
drawing, unconscious, 99
dream(s), 43, 46, 66, 91, 140, 147, 150
  of Ariel, 141
  of baby and rosebush, 151
  of bicycle riding, 129
  of birth of baby, 106
  of black jewel, 66-67
  of chaos/chaotic, 97, 130
  of death, 106
  of flaming hair, 141
  of flying in outer space, 132-133, 138
  of flying to the moon, 102-104, 150
  of foot-square land, 130-132, 151
  of frustration, 105
  of hotel, 105
  of marriage, 104-105
  of mother, 106
  of mud, 131-136, 141, 144
  of mud-bath, 143-144
  of primitives, 142-143
  of religious symbols, 68
  of rosebush and baby, 151
  of snake, 106-107, 110

  of star in chair, 146-150
  of treasure, 66-67
  of tree, 130-132, 136

Ea, 48, 51-52, 54-55, 57, 61, 63, 65, 75-78
Eden, Garden of, 13, 21, 29-30, 67, 82-85,
    90, 97
ego, 52, 55-58, 64, 75-76, 83, 85-86, 88-
    92, 126, 134
  and archetype, 24
  and Self, 148, 150
emotion(s)/emotional, 27, 44, 57, 59, 61,
    70-71, 80-81, 84
Enlil, 48, 64
Enuma Elish, 32
Eros, 28, 104, 113, 115, 118
Error, 22, 90, 129
evolution of consciousness, 95
"examine the carcass," 72
eye, 136-138, 141-142, 146

fairy tale(s), 12
familiar, 50-51
Fate(s), 43, 72
father(hood), 37, 87, 92
  double, 55
Father archetype, 27-28, 37, 55, 79, 97,
    113, 115, 124, 126, 128
feminine, 27-28, 31, 50, 55-56, 58, 74,
    107, 110, 113, 115-117, 124, 149
Fierz-David, Linda, 28
  Women's Dionysian Initiation, 35
fire, 117, 146
first beginnings, 20-21
first half of life, 124
First World War, 73
flaming hair, dream of, 141
flood(s), 39-40. *See also* river(s); water(s)
flying, to moon, dream of, 102-104, 150
  in outer space, dream of, 132-133, 138
foot-square land, dream of, 130-132, 151
free will, 44-45, 72
freedom, 71, 90, 92
Freud, S./Freudian, 59, 70
frustration, dreams of, 105

Garden of Eden, 13, 21, 23, 29-30, 67, 82-
85, 90, 97
Genesis, 28-29, 41, 43, 53, 63, 82-83
Gnostic myth, 22
god(s), 21, 23, 26-28, 32-33, 35, 37-39, 41,
43-47, 53, 72, 74-76, 79-82, 84, 87,
89-90, 126-127, 130-131, 139, 151
God/God-image, 13, 23-25, 30-31, 37, 53,
77, 82-88, 93-94, 96, 101, 113, 115-
118, 121, 126-128, 132, 134, 140-141
eye of, 136, 138, 141
godparent(s), 55
Gospel According to Thomas, 149-151
Gospel of Truth, 90, 127-128, 132
Grail legend, 14
Great Mother, 15, 25, 105, 118, 124, 128

half-sister, 58, 77
head, 52
healing, of injured parental image, 99-118
heart, 143, 146, 148
Hell, 144
Herakles, 69
hero(es)/heroic, 26-27, 44-45, 54-55, 59,
62, 64, 71, 74, 88-89, 92, 124-125
struggle of, 21, 23-25, 30 , 43, 67, 78-
79, 86, 121, 134, 138
history, 95, 127
home, archetype of, 18
horoscope(s), 46
hostile brothers, 85
hotel, dream of, 105
hunting, 82-83

I Ching, 45
image, mother, 90-91
parental, 7-8, 18, 20, 66, 86-98, 118,
123, 150-151
healing injured, 99-118, 150
incarnations, previous, 22
independence, 83, 91
individuation, 14, 118, 121, 127
and reconstruction, 129-151
infinite, 39, 88
inflation, 150

initiation, 28, 144
injured archetype(s), 13, 19, 24-25, 29, 31,
66-68, 78-79, 85-87, 89-98, 118, 127,
138-139
healing, 99-118, 150
injury, 14
to God-image, 30-31
normal vs. pathological, 19, 121
innocence, 29
insight, 116
instinct(s), 14, 46, 56, 59, 70, 80, 89

jewel, black, dream of, 67
Job (Bible), 30, 38
John, 132-138, 140-143, 151
Jung, C.G., 12, 68
"Analytical Psychology and
'Weltanschauung,' " 15-17
on angels, 80
"Answer to Job," 43
"Archetypes of the Collective
Unconscious," 11
on becoming conscious, 121-122
on Brother Klaus, 140
C.G. Jung Letters, vol. 1, 118n
on chaos, 130
on decisive question, 17
on dreams, 43
on the infinite, 39, 88
Memories, Dreams, Reflections, 17, 39,
88, 92
on moral judgment, 92
on mother-child relationship, 15-16
Mysterium Coniunctionis, 94
Psychology and Alchemy, 132
"Psychology and Poetry," 130
on urge to reflection, 81
Jung Codex, 90n

Kierkegaard, Soren, 85
King, 93, 151
Kingu, 59-60, 65, 71-72, 74-77, 80
knight, 110, 115

law, 77, 89, 92

Studies in Jungian Psychology
by Jungian Analysts

Quality Paperbacks

Prices and payment in $US (except in Canada, $Cdn)

Creating a Life: Finding Your Individual Path
James Hollis (Houston) ISBN 0-919123-93-7. 160 pp. $16

Jung and Yoga: The Psyche-Body Connection
Judith Harris (London, Ontario) ISBN 0-919123-95-3. 160 pp. $16

The Creation of Consciousness: Jung's Myth for Modern Man
Edward F. Edinger (Los Angeles) ISBN 0-919123-13-9. 10 illustrations. 128 pp. $16

Conscious Femininity: Interviews with Marion Woodman
Introduction by Marion Woodman (Toronto) ISBN 0-919123-59-7. 160 pp. $16

The Middle Passage: From Misery to Meaning in Midlife
James Hollis (Houston) ISBN 0-919123-60-0. 128 pp. $16

Eros and Pathos: Shades of Love and Suffering
Aldo Carotenuto (Rome) ISBN 0-919123-39-2. 144 pp. $16

Descent to the Goddess: A Way of Initiation for Women
Sylvia Brinton Perera (New York) ISBN 0-919123-05-8. 112 pp. $16

Addiction to Perfection: The Still Unravished Bride
Marion Woodman (Toronto) ISBN 0-919123-11-2. Illustrated. 208 pp. $18pb/$25hc

The Illness That We Are: A Jungian Critique of Christianity
John P. Dourley (Ottawa) ISBN 0-919123-16-3. 128 pp. $16

Coming To Age: The Croning Years and Late-Life Transformation
Jane R. Prétat (Providence) ISBN 0-919123-63-5. 144 pp. $16

Jungian Dream Interpretation: A Handbook of Theory and Practice
James A. Hall, M.D. (Dallas) ISBN 0-919123-12-0. 128 pp. $16

Phallos: Sacred Image of the Masculine
Eugene Monick (Scranton) ISBN 0-919123-26-0. 30 illustrations. 144 pp. $16

The Sacred Prostitute: Eternal Aspect of the Feminine
Nancy Qualls-Corbett (Birmingham) ISBN 0-919123-31-7. 20 illustrations. 176 pp. $18

Close Relationships: Family, Friendship, Marriage
Eleanor Bertine (New York) ISBN 0-919123-46-5. 160 pp. $16

The Eden Project: In Search of the Magical Other
James Hollis (Houston) ISBN 0-919123-80-5. 160 pp. $16

Discounts: any 3-5 books, 10%; 6-9 books, 20%; 10 or more, 25%
Add Postage/Handling: 1-2 books, $3 surface ($6 air); 3-4 books, $5 surface ($10 air);
  5-9 books, $10 surface ($15 air); 10 or more, free surface ($20 air)

Ask for **Jung at Heart** newsletter and free Catalogue of **over 90 titles**

INNER CITY BOOKS
Box 1271, Station Q, Toronto, ON M4T 2P4, Canada

Tel. (416) 927-0355 / Fax (416) 924-1814 / E-mail: sales@innercitybooks.net